TSI MATH FOR BEGINNERS

The Ultimate Step by Step Guide to Preparing for the TSI Math Test

By

Reza Nazari

All inquiries should be addressed to:
info@effortlessMath.com
www.EffortlessMath.com

ISBN: 978-1-64612-956-0

Published by: **Effortless Math Education Inc.**

For Online Math Practice Visit www.EffortlessMath.com

Welcome to
TSI Math Prep
2023

Thank you for choosing Effortless Math for your TSI Math test preparation and congratulations on making the decision to take the TSI test! It's a remarkable move you are taking, one that shouldn't be diminished in any capacity. That's why you need to use every tool possible to ensure you succeed on the test with the highest possible score, and this extensive study guide is one such tool.

If math has never been a strong subject for you, **don't worry**! This book will help you prepare for (and even ACE) the TSI test's math section. As test day draws nearer, effective preparation becomes increasingly more important. Thankfully, you have this comprehensive study guide to help you get ready for the test. With this guide, you can feel confident that you will be more than ready for the TSI Math test when the time comes.

First and foremost, it is important to note that this book is a study guide and not a textbook. It is best read from cover to cover. Every lesson of this "self-guided math book" was carefully developed to ensure that you are making the most effective use of your time while preparing for the test. This up-to-date guide reflects the 2023 test guidelines and will put you on the right track to hone your math skills, overcome exam anxiety, and boost your confidence, so that you can have your best to succeed on the TSI Math test.

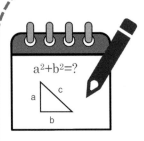

This study guide will:

☑ Explain the format of the TSI Math test.

☑ Describe specific test-taking strategies that you can use on the test.

☑ Provide TSI Math test-taking tips.

☑ Review all TSI Math concepts and topics you will be tested on.

☑ Help you identify the areas in which you need to concentrate your study time.

☑ Offer exercises that help you develop the basic math skills you will learn in each section.

☑ Give **2 realistic and full-length practice tests** (featuring new question types) with detailed answers to help you measure your exam readiness and build confidence.

This resource contains everything you will ever need to succeed on the TSI Math test. You'll get in-depth instructions on every math topic as well as tips and techniques on how to answer each question type. You'll also get plenty of practice questions to boost your test-taking confidence.

In addition, in the following pages you'll find:

➢ **How to Use This Book Effectively** – This section provides you with step-by-step instructions on how to get the most out of this comprehensive study guide.

➢ **How to study for the TSI Math Test** – A six-step study program has been developed to help you make the best use of this book and prepare for your TSI Math test. Here you'll find tips and strategies to guide your study program and help you understand TSI Math and how to ace the test.

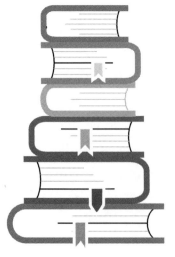

➢ **TSI Math Review** – Learn everything you need to know about the TSI Math test.

➢ **TSI Math Test-Taking Strategies** – Learn how to effectively put these recommended test-taking techniques into use for improving your TSI Math score.

➢ **Test Day Tips** – Review these tips to make sure you will do your best when the big day comes.

Effortless Math's TSI Online Center

Effortless Math Online TSI Center offers a complete study program, including the following:

✓ Step-by-step instructions on how to prepare for the TSI Math test

✓ Numerous TSI Math worksheets to help you measure your math skills

✓ Complete list of TSI Math formulas

✓ Video lessons for all TSI Math topics

✓ Full-length TSI Math practice tests

✓ And much more…

No Registration Required.

Visit **EffortlessMath.com/TSI** to find your online TSI Math resources.

How to Use This Book Effectively

Look no further when you need a study guide to improve your math skills to succeed on the math portion of the TSI test. Each chapter of this comprehensive guide to the TSI Math will provide you with the knowledge, tools, and understanding needed for every topic covered on the test.

It's imperative that you understand each topic before moving onto another one, as that's the way to guarantee your success. Each chapter provides you with examples and a step-by-step guide of every concept to better understand the content that will be on the test. To get the best possible results from this book:

- ➢ **Begin studying long before your test date**. This provides you ample time to learn the different math concepts. The earlier you begin studying for the test, the sharper your skills will be. Do not procrastinate! Provide yourself with plenty of time to learn the concepts and feel comfortable that you understand them when your test date arrives.

- ➢ **Practice consistently**. Study TSI Math concepts at least 20 to 30 minutes a day. Remember, slow and steady wins the race, which can be applied to preparing for the TSI Math test. Instead of cramming to tackle everything at once, be patient and learn the math topics in short bursts.

- ➢ Whenever you get a math problem wrong, **mark it off, and review it later** to make sure you understand the concept.

- ➢ Start each session by **looking over the previous material.**

- ➢ Once you've reviewed the book's lessons, **take a practice test at the back of the book** to gauge your level of readiness. Then, review your results. Read detailed answers and solutions for each question you missed.

- ➢ **Take another practice test** to get an idea of how ready you are to take the actual exam. Taking the practice tests will give you the confidence you need on test day. Simulate the TSI testing environment by sitting in a quiet room free from distraction. Make sure to clock yourself with a timer.

How to Study for the TSI Math Test

Studying for the TSI Math test can be a really daunting and boring task. What's the best way to go about it? Is there a certain study method that works better than others? Well, studying for the TSI Math can be done effectively. The following six-step program has been designed to make preparing for the TSI Math test more efficient and less overwhelming.

Step 1 - Create a study plan

Step 2 - Choose your study resources

Step 3 - Review, Learn, Practice

Step 4 - Learn and practice test-taking strategies

Step 5 - Learn the TSI Test format and take practice tests

Step 6 - Analyze your performance

STEP 1: Create a Study Plan

It's always easier to get things done when you have a plan. Creating a study plan for the TSI Math test can help you to stay on track with your studies. It's important to sit down and prepare a study plan with what works with your life, work, and any other obligations you may have. Devote enough time each day to studying. It's also a great idea to break down each section of the exam into blocks and study one concept at a time.

It's important to understand that there is no "right" way to create a study plan. Your study plan will be personalized based on your specific needs and learning style.

Follow these guidelines to create an effective study plan for your TSI Math test:

★ **Analyze your learning style and study habits** – Everyone has a different learning style. It is essential to embrace your individuality and the unique way you learn. Think about what works and what doesn't work for you. Do you prefer TSI Math prep books or a combination of textbooks and video lessons? Does it work better for you if you study every night for thirty minutes or is it more effective to study in the morning before going to work?

★ **Evaluate your schedule** – Review your current schedule and find out how much time you can consistently devote to TSI Math study.

★ **Develop a schedule** – Now it's time to add your study schedule to your calendar like any other obligation. Schedule time for study, practice, and review. Plan out which topic you will study on which day to ensure that you're devoting enough time to each concept. Develop a study plan that is mindful, realistic, and flexible.

★ **Stick to your schedule** – A study plan is only effective when it is followed consistently. You should try to develop a study plan that you can follow for the length of your study program.

★ **Evaluate your study plan and adjust as needed** – Sometimes you need to adjust your plan when you have new commitments. Check in with yourself regularly to make sure that you're not falling behind in your study plan. Remember, the most important thing is sticking to your plan. Your study plan is all about helping you be more productive. If you find that your study plan is not as effective as you want, don't get discouraged. It's okay to make changes as you figure out what works best for you.

STEP 2: Choose Your Study Resources

There are numerous textbooks and online resources available for the TSI Math test, and it may not be clear where to begin. Don't worry! This study guide provides everything you need to fully prepare for your TSI Math test. In addition to the book content, you can also use Effortless Math's online resources. (Video lessons, worksheets, formulas, etc.) On each

page, there is a link (and a QR code) to an online webpage which provides a comprehensive review of the topic, step-by-step instruction, video tutorial, and numerous examples and exercises to help you fully understand the concept.

Simply visit EffortlessMath.com/TSI to find your online TSI Math resources.

STEP 3: Review, Learn, Practice

This TSI Math study guide breaks down each subject into specific skills or content areas. For instance, the percent concept is separated into different topics–percent calculation, percent increase and decrease, percent problems, etc. Use this book to help you go over all key math concepts and topics on the TSI Math test.

As you read each chapter, take notes or highlight the concepts you would like to go over again in the future. If you're unfamiliar with a topic or something is difficult for you, do additional research on it. For each math topic, plenty of instructions, step-by-step guides, and examples are provided to ensure you get a good grasp of the material. You can also find video lessons on the <u>Effortless Math website</u> for each TSI Math concept.

Quickly review the topics you do understand to get a brush-up of the material. Be sure to do the practice questions provided at the end of every chapter to measure your understanding of the concepts.

STEP 4: Learn and Practice Test-taking Strategies

In the following sections, you will find important test-taking strategies and tips that can help you earn extra points. You'll learn how to think strategically and when to guess if you don't know the answer to a question. Using TSI Math test-taking strategies and tips can help you raise your score and do well on the test. Apply test taking strategies on the practice tests to help you boost your confidence.

STEP 5: Learn the TSI Test Format and Take Practice Tests

The TSI *Test Review* section provides information about the structure of the TSI test. Read this section to learn more about the TSI test structure, different test sections, the number of questions in each section, and the section time limits. When you have a prior understanding of the test format and different types of TSI Math questions, you'll feel more confident when you take the actual exam.

Once you have read through the instructions and lessons and feel like you are ready to go – take advantage of both of the full-length TSI Math practice tests available in this study guide. Use the practice tests to sharpen your skills and build confidence.

The TSI Math practice tests offered at the end of the book are formatted similarly to the actual TSI Math test. When you take each practice test, try to simulate actual testing conditions. To take the practice tests, sit in a quiet space, time yourself, and work through as many of the questions as time allows. The practice tests are followed by detailed answer explanations to help you find your weak areas, learn from your mistakes, and raise your TSI Math score.

STEP 6: Analyze Your Performance

After taking the practice tests, look over the answer keys and explanations to learn which questions you answered correctly and which you did not. Never be discouraged if you make a few mistakes. See them as a learning opportunity. This will highlight your strengths and weaknesses.

You can use the results to determine if you need additional practice or if you are ready to take the actual TSI Math test.

Looking for more?

Visit EffortlessMath.com/TSI to find hundreds of TSI Math worksheets, video tutorials, practice tests, TSI Math formulas, and much more.

Or scan this QR code.

No Registration Required.

TSI Test Review

The Texas Success Initiative Assessment, is known as the TSI (or TSIA2), is a test to determine the appropriate level of college course work for an incoming student. In essence, it is a broad and quick assessment of students' academic abilities.

The TSI test consists of three separate exams:

- Mathematics
- Reading
- Writing

The mathematics portion of the TSI test contains 20 questions. The test covers data analysis, geometry, and algebra on both intermediate and basic levels. Students are not allowed to use calculator when taking a TSI assessment. A pop-up calculator is embedded in the test for some questions.

TSI Math Test-Taking Strategies

Here are some test-taking strategies that you can use to maximize your performance and results on the TSI Math test.

#1 : USE THIS APPROACH TO ANSWER EVERY TSI MATH QUESTION

- Review the question to identify keywords and important information.

- Translate the keywords into math operations so you can solve the problem.

- Review the answer choices. What are the differences between answer choices?

- Draw or label a diagram if needed.

- Try to find patterns.

- Find the right method to answer the question. Use straightforward math, plug in numbers, or test the answer choices (backsolving).

- Double-check your work

#2 : USE EDUCATED GUESSING

This approach is applicable to the problems you understand to some degree but cannot solve using straightforward math. In such cases, try to filter out as many answer choices as possible before picking an answer. In cases where you don't have a clue about what a certain problem entails, don't waste any time trying to eliminate answer choices. Just choose one randomly before moving onto the next question.

As you can ascertain, direct solutions are the most optimal approach. Carefully read through the question, determine what the solution is using the math you have learned before, then coordinate the answer with one of the choices available to you. Are you stumped? Make your best guess, then move on.

Don't leave any fields empty! Even if you're unable to work out a problem, strive to answer it. Take a guess if you have to. You will not lose points by getting an answer wrong, though you may gain a point by getting it correct!

#3: BALLPARK

A ballpark answer is a rough approximation. When we become overwhelmed by calculations and figures, we end up making silly mistakes. A decimal that is moved by one unit can change an answer from right to wrong, regardless of the number of steps that you went through to get it. That's where ballparking can play a big part.

If you think you know what the correct answer may be (even if it's just a ballpark answer), you'll usually have the ability to eliminate a couple of choices. While answer choices are usually based on the average student error and/or values that are closely tied, you will still be able to weed out choices that are way far afield. Try to find answers that aren't in the proverbial ballpark when you're looking for a wrong answer on a multiple-choice question. This is an optimal approach to eliminating answers to a problem.

#4: BACKSOLVING

All questions on the TSI Math test will be in multiple-choice format. Many test-takers prefer multiple-choice questions, as at least the answer is right there. You'll typically have four answers to pick from. You simply need to figure out which one is correct. Usually, the best way to go about doing so is "backsolving."

As mentioned earlier, direct solutions are the most optimal approach to answering a question. Carefully read through a problem, calculate a solution, then correspond the answer with one of the choices displayed in front of you. If you can't calculate a solution, your next best approach involves "backsolving."

When backsolving a problem, contrast one of your answer options against the problem you are asked, then see which of them is most relevant. More often than not, answer choices are listed in ascending or descending order. In such cases, try out the choices B or C. If it's not correct, you can go either down or up from there.

#5 : PLUGGING IN NUMBERS

"Plugging in numbers" is a strategy that can be applied to a wide range of different math problems on the TSI Math test. This approach is typically used to simplify a challenging question so that it is more understandable. By using the strategy carefully, you can find the answer without too much trouble.

The concept is fairly straightforward–replace unknown variables in a problem with certain values. When selecting a number, consider the following:

- Choose a number that's basic (just not too basic). Generally, you should avoid choosing 1 (or even 0). A decent choice is 2.

- Try not to choose a number that is displayed in the problem.

- Make sure you keep your numbers different if you need to choose at least two of them.

- More often than not, choosing numbers merely lets you filter out some of your answer choices. As such, don't just go with the first choice that gives you the right answer.

- If several answers seem correct, then you'll need to choose another value and try again. This time, though, you'll just need to check choices that haven't been eliminated yet.

- If your question contains fractions, then a potential right answer may involve either an LCD (least common denominator) or an LCD multiple.

- 100 is the number you should choose when you are dealing with problems involving percentages.

TSI Mathematics Test – Daytime Tips

After practicing and reviewing all the math concepts you've been taught, and taking some TSI mathematics practice tests, you'll be prepared for test day. Consider the following tips to be extra-ready come test time.

Before Your Test

What to do the night before:

- **Relax!** One day before your test, study lightly or skip studying altogether. You shouldn't attempt to learn something new, either. There are plenty of reasons why studying the evening before a big test can work against you. Put it this way–a marathoner wouldn't go out for a sprint before the day of a big race. Mental marathoners–such as yourself–should not study for any more than one hour 24 hours before a TSI test. That's because your brain requires some rest to be at its best. The night before your exam, spend some time with family or friends, or read a book.

- **Avoid bright screens** - You'll have to get some good shuteye the night before your test. Bright screens (such as the ones coming from your laptop, TV, or mobile device) should be avoided altogether. Staring at such a screen will keep your brain up, making it hard to drift asleep at a reasonable hour.

- **Make sure your dinner is healthy** - The meal that you have for dinner should be nutritious. Be sure to drink plenty of water as well. Load up on your complex carbohydrates, much like a marathon runner would do. Pasta, rice, and potatoes are ideal options here, as are vegetables and protein sources.

- **Get your bag ready for test day** - The night prior to your test, pack your bag with your stationery, admissions pass, ID, and any other gear that you need. Keep the bag right by your front door.

- **Make plans to reach the testing site** - Before going to sleep, ensure that you understand precisely how you will arrive at the site of the test. If parking is something you'll have to find first, plan for it. If you're dependent on public transit, then review the schedule. You should also make sure that the train/bus/subway/streetcar you use will be running. Find out about road closures as well. If a parent or friend is accompanying you, ensure that they understand what steps they have to take as well.

The Day of the Test

- **Get up reasonably early, but not too early.**

- **Have breakfast** - Breakfast improves your concentration, memory, and mood. As such, make sure the breakfast that you eat in the morning is healthy. The last thing you want to be is distracted by a grumbling tummy. If it's not your own stomach making those noises, another test taker close to you might be instead. Prevent discomfort or embarrassment by consuming a healthy breakfast. Bring a snack with you if you think you'll need it.

- **Follow your daily routine** - Do you watch Good Morning America each morning while getting ready for the day? Don't break your usual habits on the day of the test. Likewise, if coffee isn't something you drink in the morning, then don't take up the habit hours before your test. Routine consistency lets you concentrate on the main objective—doing the best you can on your test.

- **Wear layers** - Dress yourself up in comfortable layers. You should be ready for any kind of internal temperature. If it gets too warm during the test, take a layer off.

- **Get there on time** - The last thing you want to do is get to the test site late. Rather, you should be there 45 minutes prior to the start of the test. Upon your arrival, try not to hang out with anybody who is nervous. Any anxious energy they exhibit shouldn't influence you.

- **Leave the books at home** - No books should be brought to the test site. If you start developing anxiety before the test, books could encourage you to do some last-minute studying, which will only hinder you. Keep the books far away—better yet, leave them at home.

- **Make your voice heard** - If something is off, speak to a proctor. If medical attention is needed or if you'll require anything, consult the proctor prior to the start of the test. Any doubts you have should be clarified. You should be entering the test site with a state of mind that is completely clear.

- **Have faith in yourself** - When you feel confident, you will be able to perform at your best. When you are waiting for the test to begin, envision yourself receiving an outstanding result. Try to see yourself as someone who knows all the answers, no matter what the questions are. A lot of athletes tend to use this technique–particularly before a big competition. Your expectations will be reflected by your performance.

During your test

- **Be calm and breathe deeply** - You need to relax before the test, and some deep breathing will go a long way to help you do that. Be confident and calm. You got this. Everybody feels a little stressed out just before an evaluation of any kind is set to begin. Learn some effective breathing exercises. Spend a minute meditating before the test starts. Filter out any negative thoughts you have. Exhibit confidence when having such thoughts.

- **Concentrate on the test** - Refrain from comparing yourself to anyone else. You shouldn't be distracted by the people near you or random noise. Concentrate exclusively on the test. If you find yourself irritated by surrounding noises, earplugs can be used to block sounds off close to you. Don't forget–the test is going to last several hours if you're taking more than one subject of the test. Some of that time will be dedicated to brief sections. Concentrate on the specific section you are working on during a particular moment. Do not let your mind wander off to upcoming or previous sections.

- **Try to answer each question individually** - Focus only on the question you are working on. Use one of the test-taking strategies to solve the problem. If you aren't able to come up with an answer, don't get frustrated. Simply skip that question, then move onto the next one.

- **Don't forget to breathe!** Whenever you notice your mind wandering, your stress levels boosting, or frustration brewing, take a thirty-second break. Shut your eyes, drop your pencil, breathe deeply, and let your shoulders relax. You will end up being more productive when you allow yourself to relax for a moment.

- **Optimize your breaks** - When break time comes, use the restroom, have a snack, and reactivate your energy for the subsequent section. Doing some stretches can help stimulate your blood flow.

After your test

- **Take it easy** - You will need to set some time aside to relax and decompress once the test has concluded. There is no need to stress yourself out about what you could've said, or what you may have done wrong. At this point, there's nothing you can do about it. Your energy and time would be better spent on something that will bring you happiness for the remainder of your day.

- **Redoing the test** - Did you pass the test? Congratulations! Your hard work paid off!

  If you have failed your test, though, don't worry! The test can be retaken. In such cases, you will need to follow the retake policy. You also need to re-register to take the exam again.

Contents

Chapter: **Fractions and Mixed Numbers**   **1**

1

Simplifying Fractions 2
Adding and Subtracting Fractions 3
Multiplying and Dividing Fractions 4
Adding Mixed Numbers 5
Subtracting Mixed Numbers 6
Multiplying Mixed Numbers 7
Dividing Mixed Numbers 8
Chapter 1: Practices 9
Chapter 1: Answers 12

Chapter: **Decimals**   **13**

2

Comparing Decimals 14
Rounding Decimals 15
Adding and Subtracting Decimals 16
Multiplying and Dividing Decimals 17
Chapter 2: Practices 18
Chapter 2: Answers 20

Chapter: **Integers and Order of Operations**   **21**

3

Adding and Subtracting Integers 22
Multiplying and Dividing Integers 23
Order of Operations 24
Integers and Absolute Value 25
Chapter 3: Practices 26
Chapter 3: Answers 28

Chapter: **Ratios and Proportions**   **29**

4

Simplifying Ratios 30
Proportional Ratios 31
Similarity and Ratios 32
Chapter 4: Practices 33
Chapter 4: Answers 36

Chapter: **Percentage**   **37**

5

Percent Problems 38
Percent of Increase and Decrease 39
Discount, Tax and Tip 40
Simple Interest 41
Chapter 5: Practices 42
Chapter 5: Answers 44

Chapter: **Exponents and Variables** 45

6

Multiplication Property of Exponents 46
Division Property of Exponents 47
Powers of Products and Quotients 48
Zero and Negative Exponents 49
Negative Exponents and Negative Bases 50
Scientific Notation 51
Addition and Subtraction in Scientific Notation 52
Multiplication and Division in Scientific Notation 53
Chapter **6**: Practices 54
Chapter 6: Answers 56

Chapter: **Expressions and Equations** 59

7

Simplifying Variable Expressions 60
Evaluating One Variable 61
Evaluating Two Variables 62
One–Step Equations 63
Multi–Step Equations 64
Rearrange Multi-Variable Equations 65
Finding Midpoint 66
Finding the Distance between Two Points 67
Chapter 7: Practices 68
Chapter 7: Answers 71

Chapter: **Linear Functions** 73

8

Finding Slope 74
Writing Linear Equations 75
Graphing Linear Inequalities 76
Write an Equation from a Graph 77
Slope-intercept Form and Point-slope Form 78
Write a Point-slope Form Equation from a Graph 79
Find $x-$ and $y-$intercepts in the Standard Form of Equation 80
Graph an Equation in the Standard Form 81
Equations of Horizontal and Vertical lines 82
Graph a Horizontal or Vertical line 83
Graph an Equation in Point-Slope Form 84
Equation of Parallel and Perpendicular Lines 85
Compare Linear Function's Graph and Equations 86
Graphing Absolute Value Equations 87
Two-variable Linear Equation Word Problems 88
Chapter 8: Practices 89
Chapter 8: Answers 96

Chapter: **Inequalities and System of Equations**   **99**

9

One–Step Inequalities 100
Multi–Step Inequalities.. 101
Compound Inequalities.. 102
Write a Linear Inequality from a Graph 103
Graph Solutions to Linear Inequalities 104
Solve Advanced Linear Inequalities in Two-Variables.......... 105
Graph Solutions to Advanced Linear Inequalities................ 106
Absolute Value Inequalities 107
System of Equations 108
Find the Number of Solutions to a Linear Equation 109
Write a System of Equations Given a Graph 110
Systems of Equations Word Problems 111
Solve Linear Equations' Word Problems................................ 112
Systems of Linear Inequalities 113
Write Two-variable Inequalities Word Problems.................... 114
Chapter 9: Practices... 115
Chapter 9: Answers 120

Chapter: **Quadratic**   **123**

10

Solving a Quadratic Equations.. 124
Graphing Quadratic Functions 125
Solve a Quadratic Equation by Factoring 126
Transformations of Quadratic Functions............................... 127
Quadratic Formula and the Discriminant 128
Characteristics of Quadratic Functions: Equations............... 129
Characteristics of Quadratic Functions: Graphs 130
Complete a Function Table: Quadratic Functions 131
Domain and Range of Quadratic Functions........................... 132
Factor Quadratics: Special Cases 133
Factor Quadratics Using Algebra Tiles................................... 134
Write a Quadratic Function from Its Vertex and Another Point 135
Chapter 10: Practices... 136
Chapter 10: Answers 121

Chapter: **Polynomials**   **123**

11

Simplifying Polynomials... 124
Adding and Subtracting Polynomials...................................... 125
Add and Subtract Polynomials Using Algebra Tiles............... 126
Multiplying Monomials... 127
Multiplying and Dividing Monomials 128
Multiplying a Polynomial and a Monomial............................. 129
Multiply Polynomials Using Area Models............................... 130
Multiplying Binomials.. 131
Multiply two Binomials Using Algebra Tiles........................... 132

11

Factoring Trinomials 133
Factoring Polynomials 134
Use a Graph to Factor Polynomials 135
Factoring Special Case Polynomials 136
Add Polynomials to Find Perimeter 137
Chapter 11: Practices 138
Chapter 11: Answers 141

Chapter: **Relations and Functions** — 143

12

Function Notation and Evaluation 144
Adding and Subtracting Functions 145
Multiplying and Dividing Functions 146
Composition of Functions 147
Evaluate an Exponential Function 148
Match Exponential Functions and Graphs 149
Write Exponential Functions: Word Problems 150
Function Inverses 151
Domain and Range of Relations 152
Rate of Change and Slope 153
Complete a Function Table from an Equation 154
Chapter 12: Practices 155
Chapter 12: Answers 159

Chapter: **Radical Expressions** — 161

13

Simplifying Radical Expressions 162
Adding and Subtracting Radical Expressions 163
Multiplying Radical Expressions 164
Rationalizing Radical Expressions 165
Radical Equations 166
Domain and Range of Radical Functions 167
Simplify Radicals with Fractions 168
Chapter 13: Practices 169
Chapter 13: Answers 172

Chapter: **Geometry and Solid Figures**   **173**

14

The Pythagorean Theorem 174
Complementary and Supplementary angles................................. 175
Parallel lines and Transversals.. 176
Triangles 177
Special Right Triangles 178
Polygons 179
Circles 180
Trapezoids.. 181
Cubes... 182
Rectangular Prisms 183
Cylinder.. 184
Chapter 14: Practices 185
Chapter 14: Answers 188

Chapter: **Statistics**   **189**

15

Mean, Median, Mode, and Range of the Given Data 190
Pie Graph.. 191
Probability Problems 192
Permutations and Combinations.. 193
Chapter 15: Practices.. 194
Chapter 15: Answers 196

Time to test -- 197
TSI Mathematics Practice Test 1-- 199
 TSI Mathematics Practice Test 2-- 205
TSI Mathematics Practice Test Answers Key ------------------------------212
TSI Mathematics Practice Test Answers and Explanations------------ 213

CHAPTER

1 Fractions and Mixed Numbers

Math topics that you'll learn in this chapter:

- ☑ Simplifying Fractions
- ☑ Adding and Subtracting Fractions
- ☑ Multiplying and Dividing Fractions
- ☑ Adding Mixed Numbers
- ☑ Subtracting Mixed Numbers
- ☑ Multiplying Mixed Numbers
- ☑ Dividing Mixed Numbers

1

Simplifying Fractions

- A fraction contains two numbers separated by a bar between them. The bottom number, called the denominator, is the total number of equally divided portions in one whole. The top number, called the numerator, is how many portions you have. And the bar represents the operation of division.

- Simplifying a fraction means reducing it to the lowest terms. To simplify a fraction, evenly divide both the top and bottom of the fraction by $2, 3, 5, 7$, etc.

- Continue until you can't go any further.

Examples:

Example 1. Simplify $\frac{18}{30}$

Solution: To simplify $\frac{18}{30}$, find a number that both 18 and 30 are divisible by. Both are divisible by 6. Then: $\frac{18}{30} = \frac{18 \div 6}{30 \div 6} = \frac{3}{5}$

Example 2. Simplify $\frac{32}{80}$

Solution: To simplify $\frac{32}{80}$, find a number that both 32 and 80 are divisible by. Both are divisible by 8 and 16. Then: $\frac{32}{80} = \frac{32 \div 8}{80 \div 8} = \frac{4}{10}$, 4 and 10 are divisible by 2, then: $\frac{4}{10} = \frac{2}{5}$ or $\frac{32}{80} = \frac{32 \div 16}{80 \div 16} = \frac{2}{5}$

Example 3. Simplify $\frac{40}{120}$

Solution: To simplify $\frac{40}{120}$, find a number that both 40 and 120 are divisible by. Both are divisible by 40, then: $\frac{40}{120} = \frac{40 \div 40}{120 \div 40} = \frac{1}{3}$

Adding and Subtracting Fractions

- For "like" fractions (fractions with the same denominator), add or subtract the numerators (top numbers) and write the answer over the common denominator (bottom numbers).

- Adding and Subtracting fractions with the same denominator:

$$\frac{a}{b} + \frac{c}{b} = \frac{a+c}{b} \qquad \frac{a}{b} - \frac{c}{b} = \frac{a-c}{b}$$

- Find equivalent fractions with the same denominator before you can add or subtract fractions with different denominators.

- Adding and Subtracting fractions with different denominators:

$$\frac{a}{b} + \frac{c}{d} = \frac{ad+bc}{bd} \qquad \frac{a}{b} - \frac{c}{d} = \frac{ad-bc}{bd}$$

Examples:

Example 1. Find the sum. $\frac{2}{3} + \frac{1}{2} =$

Solution: These two fractions are "unlike" fractions. (They have different denominators). Use this formula: $\frac{a}{b} + \frac{c}{d} = \frac{ad+cb}{bd}$

Then: $\frac{2}{3} + \frac{1}{2} = \frac{(2)(2)+(3)(1)}{3 \times 2} = \frac{4+3}{6} = \frac{7}{6}$

Example 2. Find the difference. $\frac{3}{5} - \frac{2}{7} =$

Solution: For "unlike" fractions, find equivalent fractions with the same denominator before you can add or subtract fractions with different denominators. Use this formula: $\frac{a}{b} - \frac{c}{d} = \frac{ad-bc}{bd}$

$\frac{3}{5} - \frac{2}{7} = \frac{(3)(7)-(2)(5)}{5 \times 7} = \frac{21-10}{35} = \frac{11}{35}$

bit.ly/3nKet2X

Find more at

Multiplying and Dividing Fractions

- **Multiplying fractions:** multiply the top numbers and multiply the bottom numbers. Simplify if necessary. $\frac{a}{b} \times \frac{c}{d} = \frac{a \times c}{b \times d}$

- **Dividing fractions:** Keep, Change, Flip

- Keep the first fraction, change the division sign to multiplication, and flip the numerator and denominator of the second fraction. Then, solve!

$$\frac{a}{b} \div \frac{c}{d} = \frac{a}{b} \times \frac{d}{c} = \frac{a \times d}{b \times c}$$

Examples:

Example 1. Multiply. $\frac{2}{3} \times \frac{3}{5} =$

Solution: Multiply the top numbers and multiply the bottom numbers.
$\frac{2}{3} \times \frac{3}{5} = \frac{2 \times 3}{3 \times 5} = \frac{6}{15}$, now, simplify: $\frac{6}{15} = \frac{6 \div 3}{15 \div 3} = \frac{2}{5}$

Example 2. Solve. $\frac{3}{4} \div \frac{2}{5} =$

Solution: Keep the first fraction, change the division sign to multiplication, and flip the numerator and denominator of the second fraction.
Then: $\frac{3}{4} \div \frac{2}{5} = \frac{3}{4} \times \frac{5}{2} = \frac{3 \times 5}{4 \times 2} = \frac{15}{8}$

Example 3. Calculate. $\frac{4}{5} \times \frac{3}{4} =$

Solution: Multiply the top numbers and multiply the bottom numbers.
$\frac{4}{5} \times \frac{3}{4} = \frac{4 \times 3}{5 \times 4} = \frac{12}{20}$, simplify: $\frac{12}{20} = \frac{12 \div 4}{20 \div 4} = \frac{3}{5}$

Example 4. Solve. $\frac{5}{6} \div \frac{3}{7} =$

Solution: Keep the first fraction, change the division sign to multiplication, and flip the numerator and denominator of the second fraction.
Then: $\frac{5}{6} \div \frac{3}{7} = \frac{5}{6} \times \frac{7}{3} = \frac{5 \times 7}{6 \times 3} = \frac{35}{18}$

bit.ly/3haSiQW

Find more at

Adding Mixed Numbers

Use the following steps for adding mixed numbers:

- Add whole numbers of the mixed numbers.

- Add the fractions of the mixed numbers.

- Find the Least Common Denominator (LCD) if necessary.

- Add whole numbers and fractions.

- Write your answer in lowest terms.

Examples:

Example 1. Add mixed numbers. $2\frac{1}{2} + 1\frac{2}{3} =$

Solution: Let's rewriting our equation with parts separated, $2\frac{1}{2} + 1\frac{2}{3} = 2 + \frac{1}{2} + 1 + \frac{2}{3}$.
Now, add whole number parts: $2 + 1 = 3$
Add the fraction parts $\frac{1}{2} + \frac{2}{3}$. Rewrite to solve with the equivalent fractions. $\frac{1}{2} + \frac{2}{3} = \frac{3}{6} + \frac{4}{6} = \frac{7}{6}$. The answer is an improper fraction (numerator is bigger than denominator). Convert the improper fraction into a mixed number: $\frac{7}{6} = 1\frac{1}{6}$. Now, combine the whole and fraction parts: $3 + 1\frac{1}{6} = 4\frac{1}{6}$

Example 2. Find the sum. $1\frac{3}{4} + 2\frac{1}{2} =$

Solution: Rewriting our equation with parts separated, $1 + \frac{3}{4} + 2 + \frac{1}{2}$. Add the whole number parts:
$1 + 2 = 3$. Add the fraction parts: $\frac{3}{4} + \frac{1}{2} = \frac{3}{4} + \frac{2}{4} = \frac{5}{4}$
Convert the improper fraction into a mixed number: $\frac{5}{4} = 1\frac{1}{4}$.
Now, combine the whole and fraction parts: $3 + 1\frac{1}{4} = 4\frac{1}{4}$

bit.ly/2M4oABB

Find more at

Subtracting Mixed Numbers

Use these steps for subtracting mixed numbers.

- Convert mixed numbers into improper fractions. $a\frac{c}{b} = \frac{ab+c}{b}$

- Find equivalent fractions with the same denominator for unlike fractions. (Fractions with different denominators)

- Subtract the second fraction from the first one. $\frac{a}{b} - \frac{c}{d} = \frac{ad-bc}{bd}$

- Write your answer in lowest terms.

- If the answer is an improper fraction, convert it into a mixed number.

Examples:

Example 1. Subtract. $2\frac{1}{3} - 1\frac{1}{2} =$

Solution: Convert mixed numbers into fractions: $2\frac{1}{3} = \frac{2\times3+1}{3} = \frac{7}{3}$ and $1\frac{1}{2} = \frac{1\times2+1}{2} = \frac{3}{2}$

These two fractions are "unlike" fractions. (They have different denominators). Find equivalent fractions with the same denominator. Use this formula: $\frac{a}{b} - \frac{c}{d} = \frac{ad-bc}{bd}$

$\frac{7}{3} - \frac{3}{2} = \frac{(7)(2)-(3)(3)}{3\times2} = \frac{14-9}{6} = \frac{5}{6}$

Example 2. Find the difference. $3\frac{4}{7} - 2\frac{3}{4} =$

Solution: Convert mixed numbers into fractions: $3\frac{4}{7} = \frac{3\times7+4}{7} = \frac{25}{7}$ and $2\frac{3}{4} = \frac{2\times4+3}{4} = \frac{11}{4}$

Then: $3\frac{4}{7} - 2\frac{3}{4} = \frac{25}{7} - \frac{11}{4} = \frac{(25)(4)-(11)(7)}{7\times4} = \frac{23}{28}$

Multiplying Mixed Numbers

Use the following steps for multiplying mixed numbers:

- Convert the mixed numbers into fractions. $a\frac{c}{b} = a + \frac{c}{b} = \frac{ab+c}{b}$

- Multiply fractions. $\frac{a}{b} \times \frac{c}{d} = \frac{a \times c}{b \times d}$

- Write your answer in lowest terms.

- If the answer is an improper fraction (numerator is bigger than denominator), convert it into a mixed number.

Examples:

Example 1. Multiply. $4\frac{1}{2} \times 2\frac{2}{5} =$

Solution: Convert mixed numbers into fractions, $4\frac{1}{2} = \frac{4 \times 2 + 1}{2} = \frac{9}{2}$ and $2\frac{2}{5} = \frac{2 \times 5 + 2}{5} = \frac{12}{5}$. Apply the fractions rule for multiplication: $\frac{9}{2} \times \frac{12}{5} = \frac{9 \times 12}{2 \times 5} = \frac{108}{10} = \frac{54}{5}$
The answer is an improper fraction. Convert it into a mixed number. $\frac{54}{5} = 10\frac{4}{5}$

Example 2. Multiply. $3\frac{2}{3} \times 2\frac{5}{6} =$

Solution: Converting mixed numbers into fractions, $3\frac{2}{3} \times 2\frac{5}{6} = \frac{11}{3} \times \frac{17}{6}$
Apply the fractions rule for multiplication: $\frac{11}{3} \times \frac{17}{6} = \frac{11 \times 17}{3 \times 6} = \frac{187}{18} = 10\frac{7}{18}$

Example 3. Find the product. $5\frac{1}{4} \times 3\frac{3}{8} =$

Solution: Convert mixed numbers to fractions: $5\frac{1}{4} = \frac{21}{4}$ and $3\frac{3}{8} = \frac{27}{8}$. Multiply two fractions:

$\frac{21}{4} \times \frac{27}{8} = \frac{21 \times 27}{4 \times 8} = \frac{567}{32} = 17\frac{23}{32}$

Dividing Mixed Numbers

Use the following steps for dividing mixed numbers:

- Convert the mixed numbers into fractions. $a\frac{c}{b} = a + \frac{c}{b} = \frac{ab+c}{b}$

- Divide fractions: Keep, Change, Flip: Keep the first fraction, change the division sign to multiplication, and flip the numerator and denominator of the second fraction. Then, solve! $\frac{a}{b} \div \frac{c}{d} = \frac{a}{b} \times \frac{d}{c} = \frac{a \times d}{b \times c}$

- Write your answer in lowest terms.

- If the answer is an improper fraction (numerator is bigger than denominator), convert it into a mixed number.

Examples:

Example 1. Solve. $2\frac{1}{3} \div 1\frac{1}{2}$

Solution: Convert mixed numbers into fractions: $2\frac{1}{3} = \frac{2 \times 3 + 1}{3} = \frac{7}{3}$ and $1\frac{1}{2} = \frac{1 \times 2 + 1}{2} = \frac{3}{2}$
Keep, Change, Flip: $\frac{7}{3} \div \frac{3}{2} = \frac{7}{3} \times \frac{2}{3} = \frac{7 \times 2}{3 \times 3} = \frac{14}{9}$. The answer is an improper fraction. Convert it into a mixed number: $\frac{14}{9} = 1\frac{5}{9}$

Example 2. Solve. $3\frac{3}{4} \div 2\frac{2}{5}$

Solution: Convert mixed numbers to fractions, then solve:
$3\frac{3}{4} \div 2\frac{2}{5} = \frac{15}{4} \div \frac{12}{5} = \frac{15}{4} \times \frac{5}{12} = \frac{75}{48} = 1\frac{9}{16}$

Example 3. Solve. $2\frac{4}{5} \div 1\frac{2}{3}$

Solution: Converting mixed numbers to fractions: $2\frac{4}{5} \div 1\frac{2}{3} = \frac{14}{5} \div \frac{5}{3}$
Keep, Change, Flip: $\frac{14}{5} \div \frac{5}{3} = \frac{14}{5} \times \frac{3}{5} = \frac{14 \times 3}{5 \times 5} = \frac{42}{25} = 1\frac{17}{25}$

bit.ly/2KLPk9k
Find more at

Chapter 1: Practices

✎ Simplify each fraction.

1) $\dfrac{2}{8} =$

2) $\dfrac{5}{15} =$

3) $\dfrac{10}{90} =$

4) $\dfrac{12}{16} =$

5) $\dfrac{25}{45} =$

6) $\dfrac{42}{54} =$

7) $\dfrac{48}{60} =$

8) $\dfrac{52}{169} =$

✎ Find the sum or difference.

9) $\dfrac{3}{10} + \dfrac{2}{10} =$

10) $\dfrac{4}{9} - \dfrac{1}{9} =$

11) $\dfrac{2}{3} + \dfrac{6}{15} =$

12) $\dfrac{17}{24} - \dfrac{5}{8} =$

13) $\dfrac{7}{54} - \dfrac{1}{9} =$

14) $\dfrac{4}{5} - \dfrac{1}{6} =$

15) $\dfrac{6}{7} - \dfrac{3}{8} =$

16) $\dfrac{2}{13} + \dfrac{1}{4} =$

✎ Find the products or quotients.

17) $\dfrac{2}{9} \div \dfrac{4}{3} =$

18) $\dfrac{14}{5} \div \dfrac{28}{35} =$

19) $\dfrac{9}{25} \times \dfrac{5}{27} =$

20) $\dfrac{65}{72} \times \dfrac{12}{15} =$

✎ Find the sum.

21) $2\dfrac{1}{5} + 1\dfrac{2}{5} =$

22) $5\dfrac{1}{9} + 2\dfrac{7}{9} =$

23) $2\dfrac{3}{4} + 1\dfrac{1}{8} =$

24) $2\dfrac{2}{7} + 4\dfrac{1}{21} =$

25) $5\dfrac{3}{5} + 1\dfrac{4}{9} =$

26) $3\dfrac{3}{11} + 4\dfrac{6}{7} =$

bit.ly/3RAbyde

Solutions at

✎ **Find the difference**.

27) $5\frac{1}{3} - 4\frac{2}{3} =$

28) $4\frac{7}{10} - 1\frac{3}{10} =$

29) $3\frac{1}{3} - 2\frac{2}{9} =$

30) $6\frac{1}{2} - 3\frac{1}{3} =$

31) $4\frac{3}{4} - 2\frac{1}{28} =$

32) $4\frac{2}{7} - 3\frac{1}{6} =$

33) $5\frac{3}{10} - 3\frac{3}{4} =$

34) $6\frac{9}{20} - 2\frac{1}{3} =$

✎ **Find the products**.

35) $1\frac{1}{2} \times 2\frac{3}{7} =$

36) $1\frac{3}{4} \times 1\frac{3}{5} =$

37) $4\frac{1}{2} \times 1\frac{5}{6} =$

38) $1\frac{2}{7} \times 3\frac{1}{5} =$

39) $2\frac{1}{5} \times 5\frac{1}{2} =$

40) $2\frac{1}{2} \times 4\frac{4}{5} =$

41) $3\frac{1}{5} \times 4\frac{1}{2} =$

42) $4\frac{9}{10} \times 4\frac{1}{2} =$

✎ **Solve**.

43) $1\frac{1}{3} \div 1\frac{2}{3} =$

44) $2\frac{1}{4} \div 1\frac{1}{2} =$

45) $5\frac{1}{3} \div 3\frac{1}{2} =$

46) $3\frac{2}{7} \div 1\frac{1}{8} =$

47) $4\frac{1}{5} \div 2\frac{2}{3} =$

48) $1\frac{2}{3} \div 1\frac{3}{8} =$

49) $4\frac{1}{2} \div 2\frac{2}{3} =$

50) $1\frac{2}{11} \div 1\frac{1}{8} =$

Chapter 1: Answers

1) $\frac{1}{4}$

2) $\frac{1}{3}$

3) $\frac{1}{9}$

4) $\frac{3}{4}$

5) $\frac{5}{9}$

6) $\frac{7}{9}$

7) $\frac{4}{5}$

8) $\frac{4}{13}$

9) $\frac{1}{2}$

10) $\frac{1}{3}$

11) $\frac{16}{15} = 1\frac{1}{15}$

12) $\frac{1}{12}$

13) $\frac{1}{54}$

14) $\frac{19}{30}$

15) $\frac{27}{56}$

16) $\frac{21}{52}$

17) $\frac{1}{6}$

18) $\frac{7}{2} = 3\frac{1}{2}$

19) $\frac{1}{15}$

20) $\frac{13}{18}$

21) $3\frac{3}{5}$

22) $7\frac{8}{9}$

23) $3\frac{7}{8}$

24) $6\frac{1}{3}$

25) $7\frac{2}{45}$

26) $8\frac{10}{77}$

27) $\frac{2}{3}$

28) $3\frac{2}{5}$

29) $1\frac{1}{9}$

30) $3\frac{1}{6}$

31) $2\frac{5}{7}$

32) $1\frac{5}{42}$

33) $1\frac{11}{20}$

34) $4\frac{7}{60}$

35) $3\frac{9}{14}$

36) $2\frac{4}{5}$

37) $8\frac{1}{4}$

38) $4\frac{4}{35}$

39) $12\frac{1}{10}$

40) 12

41) $14\frac{2}{5}$

42) $22\frac{1}{20}$

43) $\frac{4}{5}$

44) $1\frac{1}{2}$

45) $1\frac{11}{21}$

46) $2\frac{58}{63}$

47) $1\frac{23}{40}$

48) $1\frac{7}{33}$

49) $1\frac{11}{16}$

50) $1\frac{5}{99}$

bit.ly/3RAbyde

Solutions at

CHAPTER

2 Decimals

Math topics that you'll learn in this chapter:

- ☑ Comparing Decimals
- ☑ Rounding Decimals
- ☑ Adding and Subtracting Decimals
- ☑ Multiplying and Dividing Decimals

13

Comparing Decimals

- A decimal is a fraction written in a special form. For example, instead of writing $\frac{1}{2}$ you can write: 0.5

- A Decimal Number contains a Decimal Point. It separates the whole number part from the fractional part of a decimal number.

- Let's review decimal place values: Example: **45.3861**

4: tens   5: ones   3: tenths

8: hundredths   6: thousandths   1: tens thousandths

- To compare two decimals, compare each digit of two decimals in the same place value. Start from left. Compare hundreds, tens, ones, tenth, hundredth, etc.

- To compare numbers, use these symbols:

Equal to =   Less than <   Greater than >

Greater than or equal ≥   Less than or equal ≤

Examples:

Example 1. Compare 0.03 and 0.30.

Solution: 0.30 *is greater than* 0.03, because the tenth place of 0.30 is 3, but the tenth place of 0.03 is zero. Then: 0.03 < 0.30

Example 2. Compare 0.0917 and 0.217.

Solution: 0.217 *is greater than* 0.0917, because the tenth place of 0.217 is 2, but the tenth place of 0.0917 is zero. Then: 0.0917 < 0.217

Rounding Decimals

-   We can round decimals to a certain accuracy or number of decimal places. This is used to make calculations easier to do and results easier to understand when exact values are not too important.

-   First, you'll need to remember your place values: For example: **12.4869**

    1: tens   2: ones   4: tenths

    8: hundredths   6: thousandths   9: tens thousandths

-   To round a decimal, first find the place value you'll round to.

-   Find the digit to the right of the place value you're rounding to. If it is 5 or bigger, add 1 to the place value you're rounding to and remove all digits on its right side. If the digit to the right of the place value is less than 5, keep the place value and remove all digits on the right.

Examples:

Example 1. Round 4.3679 to the thousandth place value.

Solution: First, look at the next place value to the right, (tens thousandths). It's 9 and it is greater than 5. Thus add 1 to the digit in the thousandth place. The thousandth place is 7. $\rightarrow 7 + 1 = 8$, then, the answer is 4.368

Example 2. Round 1.5237 to the nearest hundredth.

Solution: First, look at the digit to the right of hundredth (thousandths place value). It's 3 and it is less than 5, thus remove all the digits to the right of hundredth place. Then, the answer is 1.52

Adding and Subtracting Decimals

- Line up the decimal numbers.

- Add zeros to have the same number of digits for both numbers if necessary.

- Remember your place values: For example: 73.5196

7: tens   3: ones   5: tenths

1: hundredths   9: thousandths   6: tens thousandths

- Add or subtract using column addition or subtraction.

Examples:

Example 1. Add. $1.7 + 4.12$

Solution: First, line up the numbers: $\begin{array}{r} 1.7 \\ +4.12 \\ \hline \end{array} \rightarrow$ Add a zero to have the same number of digits for both numbers. $\begin{array}{r} 1.70 \\ +4.12 \\ \hline \end{array} \rightarrow$ Start with the hundredths place: $0 + 2 = 2,$ $\begin{array}{r} 1.70 \\ +4.12 \\ \hline 2 \end{array} \rightarrow$ Continue with tenths place: $7 + 1 = 8,$ $\begin{array}{r} 1.70 \\ +4.12 \\ \hline .82 \end{array} \rightarrow$ Add the ones place: $4 + 1 = 5,$ $\begin{array}{r} 1.70 \\ +4.12 \\ \hline 5.82 \end{array}$ The answer is 5.82.

Example 2. Find the difference. $5.58 - 4.23$

Solution: First, line up the numbers: $\begin{array}{r} 5.58 \\ -4.23 \\ \hline \end{array} \rightarrow$ Start with the hundredths place: $8 - 3 = 5,$ $\begin{array}{r} 5.58 \\ -4.23 \\ \hline 5 \end{array} \rightarrow$ Continue with tenths place. $5 - 2 = 3,$ $\begin{array}{r} 5.58 \\ -4.23 \\ \hline .35 \end{array} \rightarrow$ Subtract the ones place. $5 - 4 = 1,$ $\begin{array}{r} 5.58 \\ -4.23 \\ \hline 1.35 \end{array}$

Multiplying and Dividing Decimals

For multiplying decimals:

- Ignore the decimal point and set up and multiply the numbers as you do with whole numbers.

- Count the total number of decimal places in both of the factors.

- Place the decimal point in the product.

For dividing decimals:

- If the divisor is not a whole number, move the decimal point to the right to make it a whole number. Do the same for the dividend.

- Divide similar to whole numbers.

Examples:

Example 1. Find the product. $0.65 \times 0.24 =$

Solution: Set up and multiply the numbers as you do with whole numbers. Line up the numbers: $\begin{array}{r} 65 \\ \times 24 \end{array}$ → Start with the ones place then continue with other digits → $\begin{array}{r} 65 \\ \times 24 \\ \hline 1,560 \end{array}$. Count the total number of decimal places in both of the factors. There are four decimals digits. (Two for each factor 0.65 and 0.24) Then: $0.65 \times 0.24 = 0.1560 = 0.156$

Example 2. Find the quotient. $1.20 \div 0.4 =$

Solution: The divisor is not a whole number. Multiply it by 10 to get 4: → $0.4 \times 10 = 4$

Do the same for the dividend to get 12. → $1.20 \times 10 = 12$

Now, divide $12 \div 4 = 3$. The answer is 3.

bit.ly/34DZ0cS

Find more at

Chapter 2: Practices

✑ **Compare. Use >, =, and <**

1) 0.5 ☐ 0.6

2) 0.9 ☐ 0.8

3) 0.1 ☐ 0.2

4) 0.02 ☐ 0.06

5) 0.05 ☐ 0.08

6) 0.12 ☐ 0.09

7) 3.2 ☐ 2.5

8) 4.8 ☐ 8.4

9) 0.005 ☐ 0.05

10) 2.02 ☐ 20.020

11) 55.100 ☐ 55.10

12) 0.44 ☐ 0.440

13) 6.01 ☐ 6.0100

14) 0.77 ☐ 77.0

✑ **Round each decimal to the nearest whole number.**

15) 5.8

16) 6.4

17) 12.3

18) 9.2

19) 7.6

20) 22.4

21) 6.8

22) 15.9

23) 13.41

24) 16.78

25) 67.58

26) 42.67

27) 55.89

28) 14.32

29) 78.88

30) 98.29

✎ **Find the sum or difference.**

31) $12.1 + 36.2 =$

32) $56.3 - 22.2 =$

33) $45.1 + 12.8 =$

34) $27.9 - 16.4 =$

35) $98.8 - 56.6 =$

36) $28.45 + 13.22 =$

37) $16.78 + 45.11 =$

38) $86.16 - 72.12 =$

39) $96.23 - 28.32 =$

40) $57.33 + 67.46 =$

41) $46.26 - 39.49 =$

42) $44.95 + 76.53 =$

43) $79.37 - 52.89 =$

44) $19.99 + 28.7 =$

45) $83.48 - 49.3 =$

46) $19.6 + 42.98 =$

✎ **Find the product or quotient.**

47) $3.3 \times 0.2 =$

48) $2.4 \div 0.3 =$

49) $8.1 \times 1.4 =$

50) $4.8 \div 0.2 =$

51) $4.1 \times 0.3 =$

52) $8.6 \div 0.2 =$

53) $9.9 \times 0.8 =$

54) $1.84 \div 0.2 =$

55) $2.1 \times 8.4 =$

56) $1.6 \times 4.5 =$

57) $9.2 \times 3.1 =$

58) $36.6 \div 1.6 =$

59) $1.91 \times 5.2 =$

60) $3.65 \times 1.4 =$

61) $24.82 \div 0.4 =$

62) $12.4 \times 4.20 =$

Chapter 2: Answers

1) <	22) 16	43) 26.48
2) >	23) 13	44) 48.69
3) <	24) 17	45) 34.18
4) <	25) 68	46) 62.58
5) <	26) 43	47) 0.66
6) >	27) 56	48) 8
7) >	28) 14	49) 11.34
8) <	29) 79	50) 24
9) <	30) 98	51) 1.23
10) <	31) 48.3	52) 43
11) =	32) 34.1	53) 7.92
12) =	33) 57.9	54) 9.2
13) =	34) 11.5	55) 17.64
14) <	35) 42.2	56) 7.2
15) 6	36) 41.67	57) 28.52
16) 6	37) 61.89	58) 22.875
17) 12	38) 14.04	59) 9.932
18) 9	39) 67.91	60) 5.11
19) 8	40) 124.79	61) 62.05
20) 22	41) 6.77	62) 52.08
21) 7	42) 121.48	

3 Integers and Order of Operations

Math topics that you'll learn in this chapter:

- ☑ Adding and Subtracting Integers
- ☑ Multiplying and Dividing Integers
- ☑ Order of Operations
- ☑ Integers and Absolute Value

21

Adding and Subtracting Integers

- Integers include zero, counting numbers, and the negative of the counting numbers. $\{\dots, -3, -2, -1, 0, 1, 2, 3, \dots\}$

- Add a positive integer by moving to the right on the number line. (You will get a bigger number)

- Add a negative integer by moving to the left on the number line. (You will get a smaller number)

- Subtract an integer by adding its opposite.

Number line

Examples:

Example 1. Solve. $(-2) - (-8) =$

Solution: Keep the first number and convert the sign of the second number to its opposite. (Change subtraction into addition. Then: $(-2) + 8 = 6$

Example 2. Solve. $4 + (5 - 10) =$

Solution: First, subtract the numbers in brackets, $5 - 10 = -5$.
Then: $4 + (-5) = \rightarrow$ change addition into subtraction: $4 - 5 = -1$

Example 3. Solve. $(9 - 14) + 15 =$

Solution: First, subtract the numbers in brackets, $9 - 14 = -5$
Then: $-5 + 15 = \rightarrow -5 + 15 = 10$

Example 4. Solve. $12 + (-3 - 10) =$

Solution: First, subtract the numbers in brackets, $-3 - 10 = -13$
Then: $12 + (-13) = \rightarrow$ change addition into subtraction: $12 - 13 = -1$

Multiplying and Dividing Integers

Use the following rules for multiplying and dividing integers:

-   $(negative) \times (negative) = positive$

-   $(negative) \div (negative) = positive$

-   $(negative) \times (positive) = negative$

-   $(negative) \div (positive) = negative$

-   $(positive) \times (positive) = positive$

-   $(positive) \div (negative) = negative$

Examples:

Example 1. Solve. $3 \times (-4) =$

Solution: Use this rule: (positive) × (negative) = negative.
Then: $(3) \times (-4) = -12$

Example 2. Solve. $(-3) + (-24 \div 3) =$

Solution: First, divide -24 by 3, the numbers in brackets, use this rule:
(negative) ÷ (positive) = negative. Then: $-24 \div 3 = -8$
$(-3) + (-24 \div 3) = (-3) + (-8) = -3 - 8 = -11$

Example 3. Solve. $(12 - 15) \times (-2) =$

Solution: First, subtract the numbers in brackets,
$12 - 15 = -3 \rightarrow (-3) \times (-2) =$
Now use this rule: (negative) × (negative) = positive $\rightarrow (-3) \times (-2) = 6$

Example 4. Solve. $(12 - 8) \div (-4) =$

Solution: First, subtract the numbers in brackets,
$12 - 8 = 4 \rightarrow (4) \div (-4) =$
Now use this rule: (positive) ÷ (negative) = negative $\rightarrow (4) \div (-4) =$
-1

Order of Operations

- In Mathematics, "operations" are addition, subtraction, multiplication, division, exponentiation (written as b^n), and grouping.

- When there is more than one math operation in an expression, use PEMDAS: (to memorize this rule, remember the phrase "Please Excuse My Dear Aunt Sally".)

  ❖ Parentheses

  ❖ Exponents

  ❖ Multiplication and Division (from left to right)

  ❖ Addition and Subtraction (from left to right)

Examples:

Example 1. Calculate. $(2 + 6) \div (2^2 \div 4) =$

Solution: First, simplify inside parentheses:
$(8) \div (4 \div 4) = (8) \div (1)$, Then: $(8) \div (1) = 8$

Example 2. Solve. $(6 \times 5) - (14 - 5) =$

Solution: First, calculate within parentheses: $(6 \times 5) - (14 - 5) = (30) - (9)$, Then: $(30) - (9) = 21$

Example 3. Calculate. $-4[(3 \times 6) \div (9 \times 2)] =$

Solution: First, calculate within parentheses:
$-4[(18) \div (9 \times 2)] = -4[(18) \div (18)] = -4[1]$
multiply -4 and 1. Then: $-4[1] = -4$

Example 4. Solve. $(28 \div 7) + (-19 + 3) =$

Solution: First, calculate within parentheses:
$(28 \div 7) + (-19 + 3) = (4) + (-16)$ Then: $(4) - (16) = -12$

Integers and Absolute Value

- The absolute value of a number is its distance from zero, in either direction, on the number line. For example, the distance of 9 and -9 from zero on number line is 9.

- The absolute value of an integer is the numerical value without its sign. (Negative or positive)

- The vertical bar is used for absolute value as in $|x|$.

- The absolute value of a number is never negative; because it only shows, "how far the number is from zero".

Examples:

Example 1. Calculate. $|14 - 2| \times 5 =$

Solution: First, solve $|14 - 2|$, $\rightarrow |14 - 2| = |12|$, the absolute value of 12 is 12, $|12| = 12$, Then: $12 \times 5 = 60$

Example 2. Solve. $\frac{|-24|}{4} \times |5 - 7| =$

Solution: First, find $|-24| \rightarrow$ the absolute value of -24 is 24. Then: $|-24| = 24$, $\frac{24}{4} \times |5 - 7| =$
Now, calculate $|5 - 7|$, $\rightarrow |5 - 7| = |-2|$, the absolute value of -2 is 2. $|-2| = 2$
Then: $\frac{24}{4} \times 2 = 6 \times 2 = 12$

Example 3. Solve. $|8 - 2| \times \frac{|-4 \times 7|}{2} =$

Solution: First, calculate $|8 - 2|$, $\rightarrow |8 - 2| = |6|$, the absolute value of 6 is 6, $|6| = 6$. Then: $6 \times \frac{|-4 \times 7|}{2}$
Now calculate $|-4 \times 7|$, $\rightarrow |-4 \times 7| = |-28|$, the absolute value of -28 is 28, $|-28| = 28$, Then: $6 \times \frac{28}{2} = 6 \times 14 = 84$

Chapter 3: Practices

✍ Find each sum or difference.

1) $-9 + 16 =$

2) $-18 - 6 =$

3) $-24 + 10 =$

4) $30 + (-5) =$

5) $15 + (-3) =$

6) $(-13) + (-4) =$

7) $25 + (3 - 10) =$

8) $12 - (-6 + 9) =$

9) $5 - (-2 + 7) =$

10) $(-11) + (-5 + 6) =$

11) $(-3) + (9 - 16) =$

12) $(-8) - (13 + 4) =$

13) $(-7 + 9) - 39 =$

14) $(-30 + 6) - 14 =$

15) $(-5 + 9) + (-3 + 7) =$

16) $(8 - 19) - (-4 + 12) =$

17) $(-9 + 2) - (6 - 7) =$

18) $(-12 - 5) - (-4 - 14) =$

✍ Solve.

19) $3 \times (-6) =$

20) $(-32) \div 4 =$

21) $(-5) \times 4 =$

22) $(25) \div (-5) =$

23) $(-72) \div 8 =$

24) $(-2) \times (-6) \times 5 =$

25) $(-2) \times 3 \times (-7) =$

26) $(-1) \times (-3) \times (-5) =$

27) $(-2) \times (-3) \times (-6) =$

28) $(-12 + 3) \times (-5) =$

29) $(-3 + 4) \times (-11) =$

30) $(-9) \times (6 - 5) =$

31) $(-3 - 7) \times (-6) =$

32) $(-7 + 3) \times (-9 + 6) =$

33) $(-15) \div (-17 + 12) =$

34) $(-3 - 2) \times (-9 + 7) =$

35) $(-15 + 31) \div (-2) =$

36) $(-64) \div (-16 + 8) =$

✍ Evaluate each expression.

37) $3 + (2 \times 5) =$

38) $(5 \times 4) - 7 =$

39) $(-9 \times 2) + 6 =$

40) $(7 \times 3) - (-5) =$

41) $(-8) + (2 \times 7) =$

42) $(9 - 6) + (3 \times 4) =$

43) $(-19 + 5) + (6 \times 2) =$

44) $(32 \div 4) + (1 - 13) =$

45) $(-36 \div 6) - (12 + 3) =$

46) $(-16 + 5) - (54 \div 9) =$

47) $(-20 + 4) - (35 \div 5) =$

48) $(42 \div 7) + (2 \times 3) =$

49) $(28 \div 4) + (2 \times 6) =$

50) $2[(3 \times 3) - (4 \times 5)] =$

51) $3[(2 \times 8) + (4 \times 3)] =$

52) $2[(9 \times 3) - (6 \times 4)] =$

53) $4[(4 \times 8) \div (4 \times 4)] =$

54) $-5[(10 \times 8) \div (5 \times 8)] =$

✍ Find the answers.

55) $|-5| + |7 - 10| =$

56) $|-4 + 6| + |-2| =$

57) $|-9| + |1 - 9| =$

58) $|-7| - |8 - 12| =$

59) $|9 - 11| + |8 - 15| =$

60) $|-7 + 10| - |-8 + 3| =$

61) $|-12 + 6| - |3 - 9| =$

62) $5 + |2 - 6| + |3 - 4| =$

63) $-4 + |2 - 6| + |1 - 9| =$

64) $|-6| \times |-7| + |2 - 8| =$

65) $|-12| \times |-3| + |4 - 28| =$

66) $|4 \times (-2)| \times |-9| =$

67) $|-3 \times 2| \times |-5| =$

68) $|3 - 12| - |-3 \times 7| =$

69) $|-9| + |-7 \times 5| =$

70) $|-11| + |-6 \times 4| =$

71) $|-4 \times 2 + 6| \times |-2 \times 8| =$

72) $|-1 \times 5 + 2| \times |-4| =$

Chapter 3: Answers

1) 7	25) 42	49) 19
2) −24	26) −15	50) −22
3) −14	27) −36	51) 84
4) 25	28) 45	52) 6
5) 12	29) −11	53) 8
6) −17	30) −9	54) −10
7) 18	31) 60	55) 8
8) 9	32) 12	56) 4
9) 0	33) 3	57) 17
10) −10	34) 10	58) 3
11) −10	35) −8	59) 9
12) −25	36) 8	60) −2
13) −37	37) 13	61) 0
14) −38	38) 13	62) 10
15) 8	39) −12	63) 8
16) −19	40) 26	64) 48
17) −6	41) 6	65) 60
18) 1	42) 15	66) 72
19) −18	43) −2	67) 30
20) −8	44) −4	68) −12
21) −20	45) −21	69) 44
22) −5	46) −17	70) 35
23) −9	47) −23	71) 32
24) 60	48) 12	72) 12

CHAPTER

4 Ratios and Proportions

Math topics that you'll learn in this chapter:

☑ Simplifying Ratios

☑ Proportional Ratios

☑ Similarity and Ratios

29

Simplifying Ratios

- Ratios are used to make comparisons between two numbers.

- Ratios can be written as a fraction, using the word "to", or with a colon. Example: $\frac{3}{4}$ or "3 to 4" or $3:4$

- You can calculate equivalent ratios by multiplying or dividing both sides of the ratio by the same number.

Examples:

Example 1. Simplify. $8:2 =$

Solution: Both numbers 8 and 2 are divisible by $2 \Rightarrow 8 \div 2 = 4$, $4 \div 2 = 2$, Then: $8:2 = 4:1$

Example 2. Simplify. $\frac{9}{33} =$

Solution: Both numbers 9 and 33 are divisible by $3 \Rightarrow 33 \div 3 = 11$, $9 \div 3 = 3$, Then: $\frac{9}{33} = \frac{3}{11}$

Example 3. There are 24 students in a class and 10 are girls. Find the ratio of girls to boys in that class.

Solution: Subtract 10 from 24 to find the number of boys in the class. $24 - 10 = 14$. There are 14 boys in the class. So, the ratio of girls to boys is $10:14$. Now, simplify this ratio. Both 14 and 10 are divisible by 2. Then: $14 \div 2 = 7$, and $10 \div 2 = 5$. In the simplest form, this ratio is $5:7$

Example 4. A recipe calls for butter and sugar in the ratio $3:4$. If you're using 9 cups of butter, how many cups of sugar should you use?

Solution: Since you use 9 cups of butter, or 3 times as much, you need to multiply the amount of sugar by 3. Then: $4 \times 3 = 12$. So, you need to use 12 cups of sugar. You can solve this using equivalent fractions: $\frac{3}{4} = \frac{9}{12}$

bit.ly/3nKwq0Z
Find more at

Proportional Ratios

- Two ratios are proportional if they represent the same relationship.

- A proportion means that two ratios are equal. It can be written in two ways: $\frac{a}{b} = \frac{c}{d}$ $a : b = c : d$

- The proportion $\frac{a}{b} = \frac{c}{d}$ can be written as: $a \times d = c \times b$

Examples:

Example 1. Solve this proportion for x. $\frac{2}{5} = \frac{6}{x}$

Solution: Use cross multiplication: $\frac{2}{5} = \frac{6}{x} \Rightarrow 2 \times x = 6 \times 5 \Rightarrow 2x = 30$

Divide both sides by 2 to find x: $x = \frac{30}{2} \Rightarrow x = 15$

Example 2. If a box contains red and blue balls in ratio of $3 : 5$ red to blue, how many red balls are there if 45 blue balls are in the box?

Solution: Write a proportion and solve. $\frac{3}{5} = \frac{x}{45}$

Use cross multiplication: $3 \times 45 = 5 \times x \Rightarrow 135 = 5x$

Divide to find x: $x = \frac{135}{5} \Rightarrow x = 27$. There are 27 red balls in the box.

Example 3. Solve this proportion for x. $\frac{4}{9} = \frac{16}{x}$

Solution: Use cross multiplication: $\frac{4}{9} = \frac{16}{x} \Rightarrow 4 \times x = 9 \times 16 \Rightarrow 4x = 144$

Divide to find x: $x = \frac{144}{4} \Rightarrow x = 36$

Example 4. Solve this proportion for x. $\frac{5}{7} = \frac{20}{x}$

Solution: Use cross multiplication: $\frac{5}{7} = \frac{20}{x} \Rightarrow 5 \times x = 7 \times 20 \Rightarrow 5x = 140$

Divide to find x: $x = \frac{140}{5} \Rightarrow x = 28$

bit.ly/37GHQxp

Find more at

Similarity and Ratios

- Two figures are similar if they have the same shape.

- Two or more figures are similar if the corresponding angles are equal, and the corresponding sides are in proportion.

Examples:

Example 1. The following triangles are similar. What is the value of the unknown side?

Example 2.

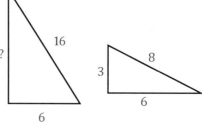

Solution: Find the corresponding sides and write a proportion.

$\frac{8}{16} = \frac{6}{x}$. Now, use the cross product to solve for x:

$\frac{8}{16} = \frac{6}{x} \rightarrow 8 \times x = 16 \times 6 \rightarrow 8x = 96$. Divide both sides by 8. Then: $8x = 96 \rightarrow x = \frac{96}{8} \rightarrow x = 12$

The missing side is 12.

Example 3. Two rectangles are similar. The first is 5 feet wide and 15 feet long. The second is 10 feet wide. What is the length of the second rectangle?

Solution: Let's put x for the length of the second rectangle. Since two rectangles are similar, their corresponding sides are in proportion. Write a proportion and solve for the missing number.

$\frac{5}{10} = \frac{15}{x} \rightarrow 5x = 10 \times 15 \rightarrow 5x = 150 \rightarrow x = \frac{150}{5} = 30$

The length of the second rectangle is 30 feet.

Chapter 4: Practices

✎ Reduce each ratio.

1) $2 : 18 = $ ___ : ___

2) $5 : 35 = $ ___ : ___

3) $8 : 72 = $ ___ : ___

4) $24 : 36 = $ ___ : ___

5) $25 : 40 = $ ___ : ___

6) $40 : 72 = $ ___ : ___

7) $28 : 63 = $ ___ : ___

8) $18 : 81 = $ ___ : ___

9) $13 : 52 = $ ___ : ___

10) $56 : 72 = $ ___ : ___

11) $42 : 63 = $ ___ : ___

12) $32 : 96 = $ ___ : ___

✎ Solve.

13) Bob has 16 red cards and 20 green cards. What is the ratio of Bob's red cards to his green cards? _____

14) In a party, 34 soft drinks are required for every 20 guests. If there are 260 guests, how many soft drinks are required? _____

15) Sara has 56 blue pens and 28 black pens. What is the ratio of Sara's black pens to her blue pens? _____

16) In Jack's class, 48 of the students are tall and 20 are short. In Michael's class 28 students are tall and 12 students are short. Which class has a higher ratio of tall to short students? _____

17) The price of 6 apples at the Quick Market is $1.52. The price of 5 of the same apples at Walmart is $1.32. Which place is the better buy? _____

18) The bakers at a Bakery can make 180 bagels in 6 hours. How many bagels can they bake in 16 hours? What is that rate per hour? _____

19) You can buy 6 cans of green beans at a supermarket for $3.48. How much does it cost to buy 38 cans of green beans?
_____

bit.ly/3RAbyde

Solutions at

✎ **Solve each proportion.**

20) $\frac{3}{2} = \frac{9}{x} \Rightarrow x = $ _____   31) $\frac{4}{18} = \frac{2}{x} \Rightarrow x = $ _____

21) $\frac{7}{2} = \frac{x}{4} \Rightarrow x = $ _____   32) $\frac{6}{16} = \frac{3}{x} \Rightarrow x = $ _____

22) $\frac{1}{3} = \frac{2}{x} \Rightarrow x = $ _____   33) $\frac{2}{5} = \frac{x}{20} \Rightarrow x = $ _____

23) $\frac{1}{4} = \frac{5}{x} \Rightarrow x = $ _____   34) $\frac{28}{8} = \frac{x}{2} \Rightarrow x = $ _____

24) $\frac{9}{6} = \frac{x}{2} \Rightarrow x = $ _____   35) $\frac{3}{5} = \frac{x}{15} \Rightarrow x = $ _____

25) $\frac{3}{6} = \frac{5}{x} \Rightarrow x = $ _____   36) $\frac{2}{7} = \frac{x}{14} \Rightarrow x = $ _____

26) $\frac{7}{x} = \frac{2}{6} \Rightarrow x = $ _____   37) $\frac{x}{18} = \frac{3}{2} \Rightarrow x = $ _____

27) $\frac{2}{x} = \frac{4}{10} \Rightarrow x = $ _____   38) $\frac{x}{24} = \frac{2}{6} \Rightarrow x = $ _____

28) $\frac{3}{2} = \frac{x}{8} \Rightarrow x = $ _____   39) $\frac{5}{x} = \frac{4}{20} \Rightarrow x = $ _____

29) $\frac{x}{6} = \frac{5}{3} \Rightarrow x = $ _____   40) $\frac{10}{x} = \frac{20}{80} \Rightarrow x = $ _____

30) $\frac{3}{9} = \frac{5}{x} \Rightarrow x = $ _____   41) $\frac{90}{6} = \frac{x}{2} \Rightarrow x = $ _____

✎ **Solve each problem.**

42) Two rectangles are similar. The first is 8 *feet* wide and 32 *feet* long. The second is 12 *feet* wide. What is the length of the second rectangle?

_____

43) Two rectangles are similar. One is 4.6 *meters* by 7 *meters*. The longer side of the second rectangle is 28 *meters*. What is the other side of the second rectangle? _____

Chapter 4: Answers

1) $1:9$
2) $1:7$
3) $1:9$
4) $2:3$
5) $5:8$
6) $5:9$
7) $4:9$
8) $2:9$

9) $1:4$
10) $7:9$
11) $2:3$
12) $1:3$
13) $4:5$
14) 442
15) $1:2$

16) *Jack's class*: $\frac{48}{20} = \frac{12}{5}$ *Michael's class*: $\frac{28}{12} = \frac{7}{3}$ Jack's class has a higher ratio of tall to short student: $\frac{12}{5} > \frac{7}{3}$

17) Quick market
18) 480, 30 bagels per hour
19) $22.04
20) 6
21) 14
22) 6
23) 20
24) 3
25) 10
26) 21
27) 5
28) 12
29) 10
30) 15

31) 9
32) 8
33) 8
34) 7
35) 9
36) 4
37) 27
38) 8
39) 25
40) 40
41) 30
42) 48 *feet*
43) 18.4 *meters*

CHAPTER

5 Percentage

Math topics that you'll learn in this chapter:

☑ Percent Problems

☑ Percent of Increase and Decrease

☑ Discount, Tax and Tip

☑ Simple Interest

37

Percent Problems

- Percent is a ratio of a number and 100. It always has the same denominator, 100. The percent symbol is "%".

- Percent means "per 100". So, 20% is $\frac{20}{100}$.

- In each percent problem, we are looking for the base, or the part or the percent.

- Use these equations to find each missing section in a percent problem:

  ❖ *Base = Part ÷ Percent*

  ❖ *Part = Percent × Base*

  ❖ *Percent = Part ÷ Base*

Examples:

Example 1. What is 20% of 40?

Solution: In this problem, we have the percent (20%) and the base (40) and we are looking for the "part". Use this formula: *Part = Percent × Base*.
Then: $Part = 20\% \times 40 = \frac{20}{100} \times 40 = 0.20 \times 40 = 8$. The answer: 20% of 40 is 8.

Example 2. 25 is what percent of 500?

Solution: In this problem, we are looking for the percent. Use this equation:
$Percent = Part \div Base \rightarrow Percent = 25 \div 500 = 0.05 = 5\%$.
Then: 25 is 5 percent of 500.

Example 3. 80 is 20 percent of what number?

Solution: In this problem, we are looking for the base. Use this equation:
$Base = Part \div Percent \rightarrow Base = 80 \div 20\% = 80 \div 0.20 = 400$
Then: 80 is 20 percent of 400.

Percent of Increase and Decrease

- Percent of change (increase or decrease) is a mathematical concept that represents the degree of change over time.

- To find the percentage of increase or decrease:

  1. New Number − Original Number

  2. (The result ÷ Original Number) × 100

- Or use this formula: Percent of change = $\frac{new\ number - original\ number}{original\ number} \times 100$

- Note: If your answer is a negative number, then this is a percentage decrease. If it is positive, then this is a percentage increase.

Examples:

Example 1. The price of a shirt increases from \$30 to \$36. What is the percentage increase?

Solution: First, find the difference: $36 - 30 = 6$

Then: $(6 \div 30) \times 100 = \frac{6}{30} \times 100 = 20$. The percentage increase is 20%. It means that the price of the shirt increased by 20%.

Example 2. The price of a table decreased from \$50 to \$35. What is the percent of decrease?

Solution: Use this formula:

$Percent\ of\ change = \dfrac{new\ number - original\ number}{original\ number} \times 100 =$

$\frac{35-50}{50} \times 100 = \frac{-15}{50} \times 100 = -30$. The percentage decrease is 30. (The negative sign means percentage decrease) Therefore, the price of the table decreased by 30%.

bit.ly/3pgPQes

Find more at

Discount, Tax and Tip

- To find the discount: Multiply the regular price by the rate of discount

- To find the selling price: Original price – discount

- To find tax: Multiply the tax rate to the taxable amount (income, property value, etc.)

- To find the tip, multiply the rate to the selling price.

Examples:

Example 1. With an 20% discount, Ella saved $50 on a dress. What was the original price of the dress?

Solution: let x be the original price of the dress. Then: 20 % *of* $x = 50$. Write an equation and solve for x: $0.20 \times x = 50 \rightarrow x = \frac{50}{0.20} = 250$. The original price of the dress was $250.

Example 2. Sophia purchased a new computer for a price of $820 at the Apple Store. What is the total amount her credit card is charged if the sales tax is 5%?

Solution: The taxable amount is $820, and the tax rate is 5%. Then:
$$Tax = 0.05 \times 820 = 41$$
Final price = Selling price + Tax → *final price* = $820 + $41 = $861

Example 3. Nicole and her friends went out to eat at a restaurant. If their bill was $60.00 and they gave their server a 15% tip, how much did they pay altogether?

Solution: First, find the tip. To find the tip, multiply the rate to the bill amount. *Tip* = $60 \times 0.15 = 9$. The final price is: $60 + $9 = $69

bit.ly/2Je5lo0

Find more at

Simple Interest

- Simple Interest: The charge for borrowing money or the return for lending it.

- Simple interest is calculated on the initial amount (principal).

- To solve a simple interest problem, use this formula:

$$Interest = principal \times rate \times time \quad (I = p \times r \times t = prt)$$

Examples:

Example 1. Find simple interest for $200 investment at 5% for 3 years.

Solution: Use Interest formula:
$I = prt$ ($P = \$200$, $r = 5\% = \frac{5}{100} = 0.05$ and $t = 3$)
Then: $I = 200 \times 0.05 \times 3 = \$30$

Example 2. Find simple interest for $1,200 at 8% for 6 years.

Solution: Use Interest formula:
$I = prt$ ($P = \$1,200$, $r = 8\% = \frac{8}{100} = 0.08$ and $t = 6$)
Then: $I = 1,200 \times 0.08 \times 6 = \$576$

Example 3. Andy received a student loan to pay for his educational expenses this year. What is the interest on the loan if he borrowed $4,500 at 6% for 5 years?

Solution: Use Interest formula: $I = prt$. $P = \$4,500$, r = 6% = 0.06 and $t = 5$
Then: $I = 4,500 \times 0.06 \times 5 = \$1,350$

Example 4. Bob is starting his own small business. He borrowed $20,000 from the bank at an 8% rate for 6 months. Find the interest Bob will pay on this loan.

Solution: Use Interest formula:
$I = prt$. $P = \$20,000$, $r = 8\% = 0.08$ and $t = 0.5$ (6 months is half year). Then:

$$I = 20,000 \times 0.08 \times 0.5 = \$800$$

Chapter 5: Practices

✎ Solve each problem.

1) What is 15% of 60? ____

2) What is 55% of 800? ____

3) What is 22% of 120? ____

4) What is 18% of 40? ____

5) 90 is what percent of 200? ____%

6) 30 is what percent of 150? ____%

7) 14 is what percent of 250? ____%

8) 60 is what percent of 300? ____%

9) 30 is 120 percent of what number? ____

10) 120 is 20 percent of what number? ____

11) 15 is 5 percent of what number? ____

12) 22 is 20% of what number? ____

✎ Solve each problem.

13) Bob got a raise, and his hourly wage increased from $15 to $21. What is the percent increase? _____ %

14) The price of a pair of shoes increases from $32 to $36. What is the percent increase? ___ %

15) At a coffee shop, the price of a cup of coffee increased from $1.35 to $1.62. What is the percent increase in the cost of the coffee? _____ %

16) A $45 shirt now selling for $36 is discounted by what percent? _____ %

17) Joe scored 30 out of 35 marks in Algebra, 20 out of 30 marks in science and 58 out of 70 marks in mathematics. In which subject his percentage of marks is best? _____

18) Emma purchased a computer for $420. The computer is regularly priced at $480. What was the percent discount Emma received on the computer? _____

19) A chemical solution contains 15% alcohol. If there is 54 ml of alcohol, what is the volume of the solution? _____

✍ Find the selling price of each item.

20) Original price of a computer: $600

Tax: 8%, Selling price: $_____

21) Original price of a laptop: $450

Tax: 10%, Selling price: $_____

22) Nicolas hired a moving company. The company charged $500 for its services, and Nicolas gives the movers a 14% tip. How much does Nicolas tip the movers? $_____

23) Mason has lunch at a restaurant and the cost of his meal is $40. Mason wants to leave a 20% tip. What is Mason's total bill, including tip? $_____

✍ Determine the simple interest for the following loans.

24) $1,000 *at* 5% *for* 4 *years.* $___

25) $400 *at* 3% *for* 5 *years.* $___

26) $240 *at* 4% *for* 3 *years.* $___

27) $500 at 4.5% for 6 years. $___

✍ Solve.

28) A new car, valued at $20,000, depreciates at 8% per year. What is the value of the car one year after purchase? $_____

29) Sara puts $7,000 into an investment yielding 3% annual simple interest; she left the money in for five years. How much interest does Sara get at the end of those five years? $_____

Chapter 5: Answers

1) 9

2) 440

3) 26.4

4) 7.2

5) 45%

6) 20%

7) 5.6%

8) 20%

9) 25

10) 600

11) 300

12) 110

13) 40%

14) 12.5%

15) 20%

16) 20%

17) Algebra

18) 12.5%

19) 360 ml

20) $648.00

21) $495.00

22) $70.00

23) $48.00

24) $200.00

25) $60.00

26) $28.80

27) $135.00

28) $18.400

29) $1,050

6 Exponents and Variables

Math topics that you'll learn in this chapter:

- ☑ Multiplication Property of Exponents
- ☑ Division Property of Exponents
- ☑ Powers of Products and Quotients
- ☑ Zero and Negative Exponents
- ☑ Negative Exponents and Negative Bases
- ☑ Scientific Notation
- ☑ Addition and Subtraction in Scientific Notation
- ☑ Multiplication and division in Scientific Notation

45

Multiplication Property of Exponents

- Exponents are shorthand for repeated multiplication of the same number by itself. For example, instead of 2×2, we can write 2^2. For $3 \times 3 \times 3 \times 3$, we can write 3^4.

- In algebra, a variable is a letter used to stand for a number. The most common letters are: x, y, z, a, b, c, m, and n.

- Exponent's rules: $x^a \times x^b = x^{a+b}$, $\frac{x^a}{x^b} = x^{a-b}$.

$$(x^a)^b = x^{a \times b} \qquad\qquad (xy)^a = x^a \times y^a \qquad\qquad \left(\frac{a}{b}\right)^c = \frac{a^c}{b^c}$$

Examples:

Example 1. Multiply. $2x^2 \times 3x^4$

Solution: Use Exponent's rules: $x^a \times x^b = x^{a+b} \rightarrow x^2 \times x^4 = x^{2+4} = x^6$.
Then: $2x^2 \times 3x^4 = 6x^6$.

Example 2. Simplify. $(x^4 y^2)^2$

Solution: Use Exponent's rules: $(x^a)^b = x^{a \times b}$.
Then: $(x^4 y^2)^2 = x^{4 \times 2} y^{2 \times 2} = x^8 y^4$.

Example 3. Multiply. $5x^8 \times 6x^5$

Solution: Use Exponent's rules: $x^a \times x^b = x^{a+b} \rightarrow x^8 \times x^5 = x^{8+5} = x^{13}$.
Then: $5x^8 \times 6x^5 = 30x^{13}$.

Example 4. Simplify. $(x^4 y^7)^3$

Solution: Use Exponent's rules: $(x^a)^b = x^{a \times b}$.
Then: $(x^4 y^7)^3 = x^{4 \times 3} y^{7 \times 3} = x^{12} y^{21}$.

Example 5. Simplify. $(x^3 y^5)^2$

Solution: Use Exponent's rules: $(x^a)^b = x^{a \times b}$.
Then: $(x^3 y^5)^2 = x^{3 \times 2} y^{5 \times 2} = x^6 y^{10}$.

bit.ly/34AWHr1

Find more at

Division Property of Exponents

For division of exponents use following formulas:

- $\dfrac{x^a}{x^b} = x^{a-b}$ $(x \neq 0)$

- $\dfrac{x^a}{x^b} = \dfrac{1}{x^{b-a}}$ $(x \neq 0)$

- $\dfrac{1}{x^b} = x^{-b}$

Examples:

Example 1. Simplify. $\dfrac{16x^3y}{2xy^2} =$

Solution: First, cancel the common factor: $2 \rightarrow \dfrac{16x^3y}{2xy^2} = \dfrac{8x^3y}{xy^2}$.

Use Exponent's rules: $\dfrac{x^a}{x^b} = x^{a-b} \rightarrow \dfrac{x^3}{x} = x^{3-1} = x^2$ and $\dfrac{x^a}{x^b} = \dfrac{1}{x^{b-a}} \rightarrow \dfrac{y}{y^2} = \dfrac{1}{y^{2-1}} = \dfrac{1}{y}$.

Then: $\dfrac{16x^3y}{2xy^2} = \dfrac{8x^2}{y}$.

Example 2. Simplify. $\dfrac{24x^8}{3x^6} =$

Solution: Use Exponent's rules: $\dfrac{x^a}{x^b} = x^{a-b} \rightarrow \dfrac{x^8}{x^6} = x^{8-6} = x^2$.

Then: $\dfrac{24x^8}{3x^6} = 8x^2$.

Example 3. Simplify. $\dfrac{7x^4y^2}{28x^3y} =$

Solution: First, cancel the common factor: $7 \rightarrow \dfrac{x^4y^2}{4x^3y}$.

Use Exponent's rules: $\dfrac{x^a}{x^b} = x^{a-b} \rightarrow \dfrac{x^4}{x^3} = x^{4-3} = x$ and $\dfrac{y^2}{y} = y$.

Then: $\dfrac{7x^4y^2}{28x^3y} = \dfrac{xy}{4}$.

Example 4. Simplify. $\dfrac{8x^3y}{40x^2y^3} =$

Solution: First, cancel the common factor: $8 \rightarrow \dfrac{8x^3y}{40x^2y^3} = \dfrac{x^3y}{5x^2y^3}$.

Use Exponent's rules: $\dfrac{x^a}{x^b} = x^{a-b} \rightarrow \dfrac{x^3}{x^2} = x^{3-2} = x$.

Then: $\dfrac{8x^3y}{40x^2y^3} = \dfrac{xy}{5y^3} \rightarrow$ now cancel the common factor: $y \rightarrow \dfrac{xy}{5y^3} = \dfrac{x}{5y^2}$.

bit.ly/37JAcIZ

Find more at

Powers of Products and Quotients

-   For any non-zero numbers a and b and any integer x, $(ab)^x = a^x \times b^x$ and $\left(\frac{a}{b}\right)^c = \frac{a^c}{b^c}$.

Examples:

Example 1. Simplify. $(3x^3y^2)^2$

Solution: Use Exponent's rules: $(x^a)^b = x^{a \times b}$.

$$(3x^3y^2)^2 = (3)^2(x^3)^2(y^2)^2 = 9x^{3 \times 2}y^{2 \times 2} = 9x^6y^4.$$

Example 2. Simplify. $\left(\frac{2x^3}{3x^2}\right)^2$

Solution: First, cancel the common factor: $x \rightarrow \left(\frac{2x^3}{3x^2}\right) = \left(\frac{2x}{3}\right)^2$.

Use Exponent's rules: $\left(\frac{a}{b}\right)^c = \frac{a^c}{b^c}$. Then:

$$\left(\frac{2x}{3}\right)^2 = \frac{(2x)^2}{(3)^2} = \frac{4x^2}{9}.$$

Example 3. Simplify. $(6x^2y^4)^2$

Solution: Use Exponent's rules: $(x^a)^b = x^{a \times b}$.

$$(6x^2y^4)^2 = (6)^2(x^2)^2(y^4)^2 = 36x^{2 \times 2}y^{4 \times 2} = 36x^4y^8.$$

Example 4. Simplify. $\left(-4x^3y^5\right)^2$

Solution: Use Exponent's rules: $(x^a)^b = x^{a \times b}$.

$$\left(-4x^3y^5\right)^2 = (-4)^2(x^3)^2\left(y^5\right)^2 = 16x^{3 \times 2}y^{5 \times 2} = 16x^6y^{10}.$$

Example 5. Simplify. $\left(\frac{5x}{4x^2}\right)^2$

Solution: First, cancel the common factor: $x \rightarrow \left(\frac{5x}{4x^2}\right)^2 = \left(\frac{5}{4x}\right)^2$.

Use Exponent's rules: $\left(\frac{a}{b}\right)^c = \frac{a^c}{b^c}$. Then:

$$\left(\frac{5}{4x}\right)^2 = \frac{5^2}{(4x)^2} = \frac{25}{16x^2}.$$

Zero and Negative Exponents

- Zero-Exponent Rule: $a^0 = 1$, this means that anything raised to the zero power is 1. For example: $(5xy)^0 = 1$. (Number zero is an exception: $0^0 = 0$.)

- A negative exponent simply means that the base is on the wrong side of the fraction line, so you need to flip the base to the other side. For instance, "x^{-2}" (pronounced as "ecks to the minus two") just means "x^2" but underneath, as in $\frac{1}{x^2}$.

Examples:

Example 1. Evaluate. $\left(\frac{4}{5}\right)^{-2} =$

Solution: Use negative exponent's rule:

$$\left(\frac{x^a}{x^b}\right)^{-2} = \left(\frac{x^b}{x^a}\right)^2 \rightarrow \left(\frac{4}{5}\right)^{-2} = \left(\frac{5}{4}\right)^2.$$

Then: $\left(\frac{5}{4}\right)^2 = \frac{5^2}{4^2} = \frac{25}{16}$.

Example 2. Evaluate. $\left(\frac{3}{2}\right)^{-3} =$

Solution: Use negative exponent's rule:

$$\left(\frac{x^a}{x^b}\right)^{-3} = \left(\frac{x^b}{x^a}\right)^3 \rightarrow \left(\frac{3}{2}\right)^{-3} = \left(\frac{2}{3}\right)^3 =.$$

Then: $\left(\frac{2}{3}\right)^3 = \frac{2^3}{3^3} = \frac{8}{27}$.

Example 3. Evaluate. $\left(\frac{a}{b}\right)^0 =$

Solution: Use zero-exponent rule: $a^0 = 1$.

Then: $\left(\frac{a}{b}\right)^0 = 1$.

Example 4. Evaluate. $\left(\frac{4}{7}\right)^{-1} =$

Solution: Use negative exponent's rule:

$$\left(\frac{x^a}{x^b}\right)^{-1} = \left(\frac{x^b}{x^a}\right)^1 \rightarrow \left(\frac{4}{7}\right)^{-1} = \left(\frac{7}{4}\right)^1 = \frac{7}{4}.$$

bit.ly/3rnkh4v

Find more at

Negative Exponents and Negative Bases

- A negative exponent is the reciprocal of that number with a positive exponent. $(3)^{-2} = \frac{1}{3^2}$.

- To simplify a negative exponent, make the power positive!

- The parenthesis is important! -5^{-2} is not the same as $(-5)^{-2}$:

$$-5^{-2} = -\frac{1}{5^2} \text{ and } (-5)^{-2} = +\frac{1}{5^2}$$

Examples:

Example 1. Simplify. $\left(\frac{2a}{3c}\right)^{-2} =$

Solution: Use negative exponent's rule:
$$\left(\frac{x^a}{x^b}\right)^{-2} = \left(\frac{x^b}{x^a}\right)^2 \rightarrow \left(\frac{2a}{3c}\right)^{-2} = \left(\frac{3c}{2a}\right)^2.$$
Now, use the exponent's rule:
$$\left(\frac{a}{b}\right)^c = \frac{a^c}{b^c} \rightarrow \left(\frac{3c}{2a}\right)^2 = \frac{3^2c^2}{2^2a^2}.$$
Then: $\frac{3^2c^2}{2^2a^2} = \frac{9c^2}{4a^2}$.

Example 2. Simplify. $\left(\frac{x}{4y}\right)^{-3} =$

Solution: Use negative exponent's rule:
$$\left(\frac{x^a}{x^b}\right)^{-3} = \left(\frac{x^b}{x^a}\right)^3 \rightarrow \left(\frac{x}{4y}\right)^{-3} = \left(\frac{4y}{x}\right)^3.$$
Now, use the exponent's rule:
$$\left(\frac{a}{b}\right)^c = \frac{a^c}{b^c} \rightarrow \left(\frac{4y}{x}\right)^3 = \frac{4^3y^3}{x^3} = \frac{64y^3}{x^3}.$$

Example 3. Simplify. $\left(\frac{5a}{2c}\right)^{-2} =$

Solution: Use negative exponent's rule:
$$\left(\frac{x^a}{x^b}\right)^{-2} = \left(\frac{x^b}{x^a}\right)^2 \rightarrow \left(\frac{5a}{2c}\right)^{-2} = \left(\frac{2c}{5a}\right)^2.$$
Now, use the exponent's rule:
$$\left(\frac{a}{b}\right)^c = \frac{a^c}{b^c} \rightarrow = \left(\frac{2c}{5a}\right)^2 = \frac{2^2c^2}{5^2a^2}.$$
Then: $\frac{2^2c^2}{5^2a^2} = \frac{4c^2}{25a^2}$.

bit.ly/3nPROSM

Find more at

Scientific Notation

- Scientific notation is used to write very big or very small numbers in decimal form.

- In scientific notation, all numbers are written in the form of: $m \times 10^n$, where m is greater than 1 and less than 10.

- To convert a number from scientific notation to standard form, move the decimal point to the left (If the exponent of ten is a negative number), or to the right (If the exponent is positive).

Examples:

Example 1. Write 0.00024 in scientific notation.

Solution: First, move the decimal point to the right so you have a number between 1 and 10. That number is 2.4. Now, determine how many places the decimal moved in step 1 by the power of 10. We moved the decimal point 4 digits to the right. Then: $10^{-4} \rightarrow$ When the decimal is moved to the right, the exponent is negative. Then: $0.00024 = 2.4 \times 10^{-4}$.

Example 2. Write 3.8×10^{-5} in standard notation.

Solution: The exponent is negative 5. Then, move the decimal point to the left five digits. (Remember $3.8 = 0000003.8$.) When the decimal is moved to the right, the exponent is negative. Then: $3.8 \times 10^{-5} = 0.000038$.

Example 3. Write 0.00031 in scientific notation.

Solution: First, move the decimal point to the right so you have a number between 1 and 10. Then: $m = 3.1$. Now, determine how many places the decimal moved in step 1 by the power of 10. $10^{-4} \rightarrow$ Then: $0.00031 = 3.1 \times 10^{-4}$.

Example 4. Write 6.2×10^5 in standard notation.

Solution: $10^5 \rightarrow$ The exponent is positive 5.
Then, move the decimal point to the right five digits.
(Remember $6.2 = 6.20000$.) Then: $6.2 \times 10^5 = 620,000$.

Find more at bit.ly/3nOwJYP

Addition and Subtraction in Scientific Notation

- To add or subtract numbers in scientific notions, we need to have the same power as the base (number 10).

- Adding and subtracting numbers in scientific notion:

  ❖ Step 1: Adjust the powers in the numbers so that they have the same power. (It is easier to adjust the smaller power to equal the larger one.)

  ❖ Step 2: Add or subtract the numbers.

  ❖ Step 3: Convert the answer to scientific notation if needed.

Examples:

Write the answers in scientific notation.

Example 1. $3.9 \times 10^5 + 4.2 \times 10^5$

Solution: Since two numbers have the same power, factor 10^5 out.

$$(3.9 + 4.2) \times 10^5 = 8.1 \times 10^5.$$

Example 2. $7.6 \times 10^9 - 5.5 \times 10^9$

Solution: Since two numbers have the same power, factor 10^9 out.

$$(7.6 - 5.5) \times 10^9 = 2.1 \times 10^9.$$

Example 3. $6.4 \times 10^7 - 3.2 \times 10^6.$

Solution: Convert the second number to have the same power of 10.

$$3.2 \times 10^6 = 0.32 \times 10^7.$$

Now, two numbers have the same power of 10.

Subtract: $6.4 \times 10^7 - 0.32 \times 10^7 = 6.08 \times 10^7.$

Multiplication and Division in Scientific Notation

- When multiplying two numbers in scientific notation, the process involves multiplying their coefficients and adding their exponents. This way, the product of the two numbers can be expressed in a concise form that is easier to work with and understand. The result of the multiplication will also be in scientific notation, allowing for efficient computation and manipulation of large or small numbers.

- To divide two numbers in scientific notation, divide their coefficients, and subtract their exponents.

Examples:

Write the answers in scientific notation.

Example 1. $(1.2 \times 10^5)(3 \times 10^{-2}) =$

Solution: First, multiply the coefficients: $1.2 \times 3 = 3.6$.

Add the powers of 10: $10^5 \times 10^{-2} = 10^3$.

Then: $(1.2 \times 10^5)(3 \times 10^{-2}) = 3.6 \times 10^3$.

Example 2. $\frac{2.8 \times 10^{-4}}{7 \times 10^6} =$

Solution: First, divide the coefficients: $\frac{2.8}{7} = 0.4$

Subtract the power of the exponent in the denominator from the exponent in the numerator: $\frac{10^{-4}}{10^6} = 10^{-4-6} = 10^{-10}$. Then: $\frac{2.8 \times 10^{-4}}{7 \times 10^6} = 0.4 \times 10^{-10}$.

Now, convert the answer to scientific notation: $0.4 \times 10^{-10} = 4 \times 10^{-11}$.

Example 3. $(4.3 \times 10^7)(5 \times 10^9) =$

Solution: First, multiply the coefficients: $4.3 \times 5 = 21.5$

Add the powers of 10: $10^7 \times 10^9 = 10^{16}$. Then: $(4.3 \times 10^7)(5 \times 10^9) = 21.5 \times 10^{16}$.

Now, convert the answer to scientific notation: $21.5 \times 10^{16} = 2.15 \times 10^{17}$.

bit.ly/3vFo6oD

Find more at

Chapter 6: Practices

✎ Find the products.

1) $x^2 \times 4xy^2 =$

2) $3x^2y \times 5x^3y^2 =$

3) $6x^4y^2 \times x^2y^3 =$

4) $7xy^3 \times 2x^2y =$

5) $-5x^5y^5 \times x^3y^2 =$

6) $-8x^3y^2 \times 3x^3y^2 =$

7) $-6x^2y^6 \times 5x^4y^2 =$

8) $-3x^3y^3 \times 2x^3y^2 =$

9) $-6x^5y^3 \times 4x^4y^3 =$

10) $-2x^4y^3 \times 5x^6y^2 =$

11) $-7y^6 \times 3x^6y^3 =$

12) $-9x^4 \times 2x^4y^2 =$

✎ Simplify.

13) $\frac{5^3 \times 5^4}{5^9 \times 5} =$

14) $\frac{3^3 \times 3^2}{7^2 \times 7} =$

15) $\frac{15x^5}{5x^3} =$

16) $\frac{16x^3}{4x^5} =$

17) $\frac{72y^2}{8x^3y^6} =$

18) $\frac{10x^3y^4}{50x^2y^3} =$

19) $\frac{13y^2}{52x^4y^4} =$

20) $\frac{50xy^3}{200x^3y^4} =$

21) $\frac{48x^2}{56x^2y^2} =$

22) $\frac{81y^6x}{54x^4y^3} =$

✎ Solve.

23) $(x^3y^3)^2 =$

24) $(3x^3y^4)^3 =$

25) $(4x \times 6xy^3)^2 =$

26) $(5x \times 2y^3)^3 =$

27) $\left(\frac{9x}{x^3}\right)^2 =$

28) $\left(\frac{3y}{18y^2}\right)^2 =$

29) $\left(\frac{3x^2y^3}{24x^4y^2}\right)^3 =$

30) $\left(\frac{26x^5y^3}{52x^3y^5}\right)^2 =$

31) $\left(\frac{18x^7y^4}{72x^5y^2}\right)^2 =$

32) $\left(\frac{12x^6y^4}{48x^5y^3}\right)^2 =$

✎ **Evaluate each expression.**

33) $\left(\frac{1}{4}\right)^{-2} =$

34) $\left(\frac{1}{3}\right)^{-2} =$

35) $\left(\frac{1}{7}\right)^{-3} =$

36) $\left(\frac{2}{5}\right)^{-3} =$

37) $\left(\frac{2}{3}\right)^{-3} =$

38) $\left(\frac{3}{5}\right)^{-4} =$

✎ **Write each expression with positive exponents.**

39) $x^{-7} =$

40) $3y^{-5} =$

41) $15y^{-3} =$

42) $-20x^{-4} =$

43) $12a^{-3}b^5 =$

44) $25a^3b^{-4}c^{-3} =$

45) $-4x^5y^{-3}z^{-6} =$

46) $\frac{18y}{x^3y^{-2}} =$

47) $\frac{20a^{-2}b}{-12c^{-4}} =$

✎ **Write each number in scientific notation.**

48) $0.00412 =$

49) $0.000053 =$

50) $66{,}000 =$

51) $72{,}000{,}000 =$

✎ **Write the answer in scientific notation.**

52) $6 \times 10^4 + 10 \times 10^4 =$ _____

53) $7.2 \times 10^6 - 3.3 \times 10^6 =$ _____

54) $2.23 \times 10^7 + 5.2 \times 10^7 =$ _____

55) $8.3 \times 10^9 - 5.6 \times 10^8 =$ _____

56) $1.4 \times 10^2 + 7.4 \times 10^5 =$ _____

57) $9.6 \times 10^6 - 3 \times 10^4 =$ _____

✎ **Simplify. Write the answer in scientific notation.**

58) $(5.6 \times 10^{12})(3 \times 10^{-7}) =$ ____

59) $(3 \times 10^{-8})(7 \times 10^{10}) =$ ____

60) $(9 \times 10^{-3})(4.2 \times 10^6) =$ ____

61) $\frac{125 \times 10^9}{50 \times 10^{12}} =$ ____

62) $\frac{2.8 \times 10^{12}}{0.4 \times 10^{20}} =$ ____

63) $\frac{9 \times 10^8}{3 \times 10^7} =$ ____

Chapter 6: Answers

1) $4x^3y^2$

2) $15x^5y^3$

3) $6x^6y^5$

4) $14x^3y^4$

5) $-5x^8y^7$

6) $-24x^6y^4$

7) $-30x^6y^8$

8) $-6x^6y^5$

9) $-24x^9y^6$

10) $-10x^{10}y^5$

11) $-21x^6y^9$

12) $-18x^8y^2$

13) $\frac{1}{125}$

14) $\frac{243}{343}$

15) $3x^2$

16) $\frac{4}{x^2}$

17) $\frac{9}{x^3y^4}$

18) $\frac{xy}{5}$

19) $\frac{1}{4x^4y^2}$

20) $\frac{1}{4x^2y}$

21) $\frac{6}{7y^2}$

22) $\frac{3y^3}{2x^3}$

23) x^6y^6

24) $27x^9y^{12}$

25) $576x^4y^6$

26) $1,000x^3y^9$

27) $\frac{81}{x^4}$

28) $\frac{1}{36y^2}$

29) $\frac{y^3}{512x^6}$

30) $\frac{x^4}{4y^4}$

31) $\frac{x^4y^4}{16}$

32) $\frac{x^2y^2}{16}$

33) 16

34) 9

35) 343

36) $\frac{125}{8}$

37) $\frac{27}{8}$

38) $\frac{625}{81}$

39) $\frac{1}{x^7}$

40) $\frac{3}{y^5}$

41) $\frac{15}{y^3}$

42) $-\frac{20}{x^4}$

43) $\frac{12b^5}{a^3}$

44) $\frac{25a^3}{b^4c^3}$

45) $-\frac{4x^5}{y^3z^6}$

46) $\frac{18y^3}{x^3}$

47) $-\frac{5bc^4}{3a^2}$

48) 4.12×10^{-3}

49) 5.3×10^{-5}

50) 6.6×10^4

51) 7.2×10^7

52) 1.6×10^5

53) 3.9×10^6

54) 7.43×10^7

55) 7.74×10^9

56) 7.4014×10^5

57) 9.57×10^6

58) 1.68×10^6

59) 2.1×10^3

60) 3.78×10^4

61) 2.5×10^{-3}

62) 7×10^{-8}

63) 3×10^1

CHAPTER

7 Expressions and Equations

Math topics that you'll learn in this chapter:

- ☑ Simplifying Variable Expressions
- ☑ Evaluating One Variable
- ☑ Evaluating Two Variables
- ☑ One–Step Equations
- ☑ Multi–Step Equations
- ☑ Rearrange Multi-Variable Equations
- ☑ Finding Midpoint
- ☑ Finding the Distance between Two Points

59

Simplifying Variable Expressions

- In algebra, a variable is a letter used to stand for a number. The most common letters are x, y, z, a, b, c, m, and n.

- An algebraic expression is an expression that contains integers, variables, and math operations such as addition, subtraction, multiplication, division, etc.

- In an expression, we can combine "like" terms. (Values with same variable and same power.)

Examples:

Example 1. Simplify. $(4x + 2x + 4) =$

Solution: In this expression, there are three terms: $4x$, $2x$, and 4. Two terms are "like" terms: $4x$ and $2x$. Combine like terms. $4x + 2x = 6x$.
Then:
$$(4x + 2x + 4) = 6x + 4.$$
(*Remember you cannot combine variables and numbers.*)

Example 2. Simplify. $-2x^2 - 5x + 4x^2 - 9 =$

Solution: Combine "like" terms: $-2x^2 + 4x^2 = 2x^2$.
Then:
$$-2x^2 - 5x + 4x^2 - 9 = 2x^2 - 5x - 9.$$

Example 3. Simplify. $(-8 + 6x^2 + 3x^2 + 9x) =$

Solution: Combine "like" terms: $6x^2 + 3x^2 = 9x^2$.
Then:
$$(-8 + 6x^2 + 3x^2 + 9x) = 9x^2 + 9x - 8.$$

Example 4. Simplify. $-10x + 6x^2 - 3x + 9x^2 =$

Solution: Combine "like" terms: $-10x - 3x = -13x$, and $6x^2 + 9x^2 = 15x^2$.
Then:
$$-10x + 6x^2 - 3x + 9x^2 = -13x + 15x^2.$$
Write in standard form (biggest powers first):
$$-13x + 15x^2 = 15x^2 - 13x.$$

Evaluating One Variable

- To evaluate one-variable expression, find the variable and substitute a number for that variable.

- Perform the arithmetic operations.

Examples:

Example 1. Calculate this expression for $x = 2$: $8 + 2x$.

Solution: First, substitute 2 for x.
Then: $8 + 2x = 8 + 2(2)$.
Now, use the order of operation to find the answer:
$$8 + 2(2) = 8 + 4 = 12.$$

Example 2. Evaluate this expression for $x = -1$: $4x - 8$.

Solution: First, substitute -1 for x.
Then: $4x - 8 = 4(-1) - 8$.
Now, use the order of operation to find the answer:
$$4(-1) - 8 = -4 - 8 = -12.$$

Example 3. Find the value of this expression when $x = 4$. $(16 - 5x)$.

Solution: First, substitute 4 for x,
then:
$$16 - 5x = 16 - 5(4) = 16 - 20 = -4.$$

Example 4. Solve this expression for $x = -3$: $15 + 7x$.

Solution: Substitute -3 for x.
Then:
$$15 + 7x = 15 + 7(-3) = 15 - 21 = -6.$$

Example 5. Solve this expression for $x = -2$: $12 + 3x$.

Solution: Substitute -2 for x,

then: $12 + 3x = 12 + 3(-2) = 12 - 6 = 6.$

bit.ly/3ppujQZ

Find more at

Evaluating Two Variables

- To evaluate an algebraic expression, substitute a number for each variable.

- Evaluating an algebraic expression involves replacing variables in the expression with specific numerical values to obtain a single numerical value as the answer. To do this, the following steps can be followed:

  1- Substitute the given numerical values for the variables in the expression.

  2- Simplify the expression by performing the necessary arithmetic operations (addition, subtraction, multiplication, division, exponentiation, etc.) in the order prescribed by the rules of arithmetic.

  3- Continue simplifying the expression until you obtain a single numerical value as the answer.

Examples:

Example 1. Calculate this expression for $a = 2$ and $b = -1$: $(4a - 3b)$.

Solution: First, substitute 2 for a, and -1 for b.
Then: $4a - 3b = 4(2) - 3(-1)$.
Now, use the order of operation to find the answer:
$$4(2) - 3(-1) = 8 + 3 = 11.$$

Example 2. Evaluate this expression for $x = -2$ and $y = 2$: $(3x + 6y)$.

Solution: Substitute -2 for x, and 2 for y.
Then:
$$3x + 6y = 3(-2) + 6(2) = -6 + 12 = 6.$$

Example 3. Find the value of this expression $2(6a - 5b)$, when $a = -1$ and $b = 4$.

Solution: Substitute -1 for a, and 4 for b.
Then:
$$2(6a - 5b) = 2\big(6(-1) - 5(4)\big) = 2(-6 - 20) = 2(-26) = -52.$$

Example 4. Evaluate this expression. $-7x - 2y$, $x = 4$, $y = -3$.

Solution: Substitute 4 for x, and -3 for y and simplify.
Then: $-7x - 2y = -7(4) - 2(-3) = -28 + 6 = -22.$

bit.ly/2JfrzWJ

Find more at

One–Step Equations

- The values of two expressions on both sides of an equation are equal. Example: $ax = b$. In this equation, ax is equal to b.

- Solving an equation means finding the value of the variable.

- You only need to perform one Math operation to solve the one-step equations.

- To solve a one-step equation, find the inverse (opposite) operation that is being performed.

- The inverse operations are:

  - ❖ Addition and subtraction
  - ❖ Multiplication and division

Examples:

Example 1. Solve this equation for x: $4x = 16 \rightarrow x = ?$

Solution: Here, the operation is multiplication (Variable x is multiplied by 4.) and its inverse operation is division. To solve this equation, divide both sides of equation by 4:

$$4x = 16 \rightarrow \frac{4x}{4} = \frac{16}{4} \rightarrow x = 4.$$

Example 2. Solve this equation: $x + 8 = 0 \rightarrow x = ?$

Solution: In this equation, 8 is added to the variable x. The inverse operation of addition is subtraction. To solve this equation, subtract 8 from both sides of the equation:

$$x + 8 - 8 = 0 - 8.$$

Then: $x = -8$.

Example 3. Solve this equation for x. $x - 12 = 0$

Solution: Here, the operation is subtraction, and its inverse operation is addition. To solve this equation, add 12 to both sides of the equation:

$$x - 12 + 12 = 0 + 12 \rightarrow x = 12.$$

bit.ly/37Jq0tK

Find more at

Multi–Step Equations

- To solve a multi-step equation, combine "like" terms on one side.

- Bring variables to one side by adding or subtracting.

- Simplify using the inverse of addition or subtraction.

- Simplify further by using the inverse of multiplication or division.

- Check your solution by plugging the value of the variable into the original equation.

Examples:

Example 1. Solve this equation for x. $4x + 8 = 20 - 2x$

Solution: First, bring variables to one side by adding $2x$ to both sides. Then:
$$4x + 8 + 2x = 20 - 2x + 2x \rightarrow 4x + 8 + 2x = 20.$$
Simplify: $6x + 8 = 20$. Now, subtract 8 from both sides of the equation:

$6x + 8 - 8 = 20 - 8 \rightarrow 6x = 12 \rightarrow$ Divide both sides by 6:
$$6x = 12 \rightarrow \frac{6x}{6} = \frac{12}{6} \rightarrow x = 2.$$
Let's check this solution by substituting the value of 2 for x in the original equation:
$$x = 2 \rightarrow 4x + 8 = 20 - 2x \rightarrow 4(2) + 8 = 20 - 2(2) \rightarrow 16 = 16.$$
The answer $x = 2$ is correct.

Example 2. Solve this equation for x. $-5x + 4 = 24$

Solution: Subtract 4 from both sides of the equation.
$$-5x + 4 = 24 \rightarrow -5x + 4 - 4 = 24 - 4 \rightarrow -5x = 20.$$
Divide both sides by -5, then:
$$-5x = 20 \rightarrow \frac{-5x}{-5} = \frac{20}{-5} \rightarrow x = -4.$$
Now, check the solution:
$$x = -4 \rightarrow -5x + 4 = 24 \rightarrow -5(-4) + 4 = 24 \rightarrow 24 = 24.$$
The answer $x = -4$ is correct.

Rearrange Multi-Variable Equations

- In order to rearrange the multi-variable equations for each of the variables:

  • Determine the dependent variable.
  • Isolate the dependent variable on both sides of the equation.
  • By undoing the operations on both sides, write the dependent variable on one side and the other variables on the other side of the equation.

Examples:

Example 1. Make x as the subject in the equation: $\frac{1}{2}x - t = 5$.

Solution: Find x like this $\frac{1}{2}x - t = 5$. To isolate x on one side of the equation, first add t to both sides, as follows: $\frac{1}{2}x - t + t = 5 + t \rightarrow \frac{1}{2}x = t + 5$. Then multiply 2 on both sides of the equation: $2\left(\frac{1}{2}x\right) = 2(t + 5) \rightarrow x = 2t + 10$.

Example 2. Solve for a in terms of b and c: $-c + b - a = 6$.

Solution: To solve the problem, find a. By undoing the operations on both sides, isolate a on one side of the equation. Add a to both sides of the equation. So,

$$-c + b - a + a = 6 + a \rightarrow -c + b = a + 6.$$

Now, subtract 6 from both sides of the equation, then:

$$-c + b - 6 = a + 6 - 6 \rightarrow -c + b - 6 = a.$$

In this case, the above equation in terms of a becomes: $a = -c + b - 6$

Example 3. Solve $V = \frac{1}{3}\pi r^2 h$ for h.

Solution: To isolate h on both sides of the equation, just multiply the sides by the expression $\frac{3}{\pi r^2}$. Therefore, $\frac{3}{\pi r^2} \times V = \frac{3}{\pi r^2}\left(\frac{1}{3}\pi r^2 h\right) \rightarrow h = \frac{3V}{\pi r^2}$.

Example 4. Solve $y = mx + c$ for m.

Solution: Specify m as the dependent variable like this $y = mx + c$. Subtract c from both sides of the equation: $y - c = mx + c - c \rightarrow y - c = mx$. In this case, divide both sides of the obtained equation by x, so, we have:

$$\frac{y-c}{x} = \frac{mx}{x} \rightarrow m = \frac{y-c}{x}.$$

Finding Midpoint

- The middle of a line segment is its midpoint.

- The midpoint of two endpoints $A(x_1, y_1)$ and $B(x_2, y_2)$ can be found using this formula: $M\left(\frac{x_1+x_2}{2}, \frac{y_1+y_2}{2}\right)$.

Examples:

Example 1. Find the midpoint of the line segment with the given endpoints.

$(2, -4), (6,8)$

Solution: Midpoint $= \left(\frac{x_1+x_2}{2}, \frac{y_1+y_2}{2}\right) \rightarrow (x_1, y_1) = (2, -4)$ and $(x_2, y_2) = (6,8)$.

Midpoint $= \left(\frac{2+6}{2}, \frac{-4+8}{2}\right) \rightarrow \left(\frac{8}{2}, \frac{4}{2}\right) \rightarrow M(4,2)$.

Example 2. Find the midpoint of the line segment with the given endpoints.
$(-2,3), (6, -7)$

Solution: Midpoint $= \left(\frac{x_1+x_2}{2}, \frac{y_1+y_2}{2}\right) \rightarrow (x_1, y_1) = (-2,3)$ and $(x_2, y_2) = (6, -7)$.

Midpoint $= \left(\frac{-2+6}{2}, \frac{3+(-7)}{2}\right) \rightarrow \left(\frac{4}{2}, \frac{-4}{2}\right) \rightarrow M(2, -2)$.

Example 3. Find the midpoint of the line segment with the given endpoints.
$(7, -4), (1,8)$

Solution: Midpoint $= \left(\frac{x_1+x_2}{2}, \frac{y_1+y_2}{2}\right) \rightarrow (x_1, y_1) = (7, -4)$ and $(x_2, y_2) = (1,8)$.

Midpoint $= \left(\frac{7+1}{2}, \frac{-4+8}{2}\right) \rightarrow \left(\frac{8}{2}, \frac{4}{2}\right) \rightarrow M(4,2)$.

Example 4. Find the midpoint of the line segment with the given endpoints.
$(6,3), (10, -9)$

Solution: Midpoint $= \left(\frac{x_1+x_2}{2}, \frac{y_1+y_2}{2}\right) \rightarrow (x_1, y_1) = (6,3)$ and $(x_2, y_2) = (10, -9)$.

Midpoint $= \left(\frac{6+10}{2}, \frac{3-9}{2}\right) \rightarrow \left(\frac{16}{2}, \frac{-6}{2}\right) \rightarrow M(8, -3)$.

Finding the Distance between Two Points

- Use the following formula to find the distance of two points with the coordinates $A(x_1, y_1)$ and $B(x_2, y_2)$:

$$d = \sqrt{(x_2 - x_1)^2 + (y_2 - y_1)^2}$$

Examples:

Example 1. Find the distance between $(4, 2)$ and $(-5, -10)$ on the coordinate plane.

Solution: Use the distance of two points formula:

$$d = \sqrt{(x_2 - x_1)^2 + (y_2 - y_1)^2}.$$

Considering that: $(x_1, y_1) = (4, 2)$ and $(x_2, y_2) = (-5, -10)$.

Then:

$$d = \sqrt{(-5 - 4)^2 + (-10 - 2)^2} = \sqrt{(-9)^2 + (-12)^2} = \sqrt{81 + 144} = \sqrt{225} = 15.$$

Then: $d = 15$.

Example 2. Find the distance of two points $(-1, 5)$ and $(-4, 1)$.

Solution: Use the distance of two points formula:

$$d = \sqrt{(x_2 - x_1)^2 + (y_2 - y_1)^2}.$$

Since $(x_1, y_1) = (-1, 5)$, and $(x_2, y_2) = (-4, 1)$.

Then:

$$d = \sqrt{(-4 - (-1))^2 + (1 - 5)^2} = \sqrt{(-3)^2 + (-4)^2} = \sqrt{9 + 16} = \sqrt{25} = 5.$$

Then: $d = 5$.

Example 3. Find the distance between $(-6, 5)$ and $(-1, -7)$.

Solution: Use the distance of two points formula:

$$d = \sqrt{(x_2 - x_1)^2 + (y_2 - y_1)^2}.$$

According to: $(x_1, y_1) = (-6, 5)$ and $(x_2, y_2) = (-1, -7)$.

Then:

$$d = \sqrt{\left(-1 - (-6)\right)^2 + (-7 - 5)^2} = \sqrt{(5)^2 + (-12)^2} = \sqrt{25 + 144} = \sqrt{169} = 13.$$

Chapter 7: Practices

✍ Simplify each expression.

1) $(3 + 4x - 1) =$

2) $(-5 - 2x + 7) =$

3) $(12x - 5x - 4) =$

4) $(-16x + 24x - 9) =$

5) $(6x + 5 - 15x) =$

6) $2 + 5x - 8x - 6 =$

7) $5x + 10 - 3x - 22 =$

8) $-5 - 3x^2 - 6 + 4x =$

9) $-6 + 9x^2 - 3 + x =$

10) $5x^2 + 3x - 10x - 3 =$

11) $4x^2 - 2x - 6x + 5 - 8 =$

12) $3x^2 - 5x - 7x + 2 - 4 =$

13) $9x^2 - x - 5x + 3 - 9 =$

14) $2x^2 - 7x - 3x^2 + 4x + 6 =$

✍ Evaluate each expression using the value given.

15) $x = 4 \to 10 - x = \underline{\quad}$

16) $x = 6 \to x + 8 = \underline{\quad}$

17) $x = 3 \to 2x - 6 = \underline{\quad}$

18) $x = 2 \to 10 - 4x = \underline{\quad}$

19) $x = 7 \to 8x - 3 = \underline{\quad}$

20) $x = 9 \to 20 - 2x = \underline{\quad}$

21) $x = 5 \to 10x - 30 = \underline{\quad}$

22) $x = -6 \to 5 - x = \underline{\quad}$

23) $x = -3 \to 22 - 3x = \underline{\quad}$

24) $x = -7 \to 10 - 9x = \underline{\quad}$

25) $x = -10 \to 40 - 3x = \underline{\quad}$

26) $x = -2 \to 20x - 5 = \underline{\quad}$

27) $x = -5 \to -10x - 8 = \underline{\quad}$

28) $x = -4 \to -1 - 4x = \underline{\quad}$

✍ Evaluate each expression using the values given.

29) $x = 2, y = 1 \to 2x + 7y = \underline{\quad}$

30) $a = 3, b = 5 \to 3a - 5b = \underline{\quad}$

31) $x = 6, y = 2 \to 3x - 2y + 8 = \underline{\quad}$

32) $a = -2, b = 3 \to -5a + 2b + 6 = \underline{\quad}$

33) $x = -4, y = -3 \to -4x + 10 - 8y = \underline{\quad}$

✍ Solve each equation.

34) $x + 6 = 3 \rightarrow x =$ ____   39) $10 - x = -2 \rightarrow x =$ ____

35) $5 = 11 - x \rightarrow x =$ ____   40) $22 - x = -9 \rightarrow x =$ ____

36) $-3 = 8 + x \rightarrow x =$ ____   41) $-4 + x = 28 \rightarrow x =$ ____

37) $x - 2 = -7 \rightarrow x =$ ____   42) $11 - x = -7 \rightarrow x =$ ____

38) $-15 = x + 6 \rightarrow x =$ ____   43) $35 - x = -7 \rightarrow x =$ ____

✍ Solve each equation.

44) $4(x + 2) = 12 \rightarrow x =$ ____   48) $4(x + 2) = -12 \rightarrow x =$ ____

45) $-6(6 - x) = 12 \rightarrow x =$ ____   49) $-6(3 + 2x) = 30 \rightarrow x =$ ____

46) $5 = -5(x + 2) \rightarrow x =$ ____   50) $-3(4 - x) = 12 \rightarrow x =$ ____

47) $-10 = 2(4 + x) \rightarrow x =$ ____   51) $-4(6 - x) = 16 \rightarrow x =$ ____

✍ Solve.

52) $q = 2l + 2w$ for w.   54) $pv = nRT$ for T.

53) $x = 2yw$ for w.   55) $a = b + c + d$ for d.

✍ Find the midpoint of the line segment with the given endpoints.

56) $(5, 0), (1, 4)$ 60) $(4, -1), (-2, 7)$

57) $(2, 3), (4, 7)$ 61) $(2, -5), (4, 1)$

58) $(8, 1), (2, 5)$ 62) $(7, 6), (-5, 2)$

59) $(5, 10), (3, 6)$ 63) $(-2, 8), (4, -6)$

bit.ly/3RAbyde

Solutions at

🖋 Find the distance between each pair of points.

64) $(-2,8),(-6,8)$

65) $(4,-4),(14,20)$

66) $(-1,9),(-5,6)$

67) $(0,3),(4,3)$

68) $(0,-2),(5,10)$

69) $(4,3),(7,-1)$

70) $(2,6),(10,-9)$

71) $(3,3),(6,-1)$

72) $(-2,-12),(14,18)$

73) $(2,-2),(12,22)$

Chapter 7: Answers

1) $4x + 2$

2) $-2x + 2$

3) $7x - 4$

4) $8x - 9$

5) $-9x + 5$

6) $-3x - 4$

7) $2x - 12$

8) $-3x^2 + 4x - 11$

9) $9x^2 + x - 9$

10) $5x^2 - 7x - 3$

11) $4x^2 - 8x - 3$

12) $3x^2 - 12x - 2$

13) $9x^2 - 6x - 6$

14) $-x^2 - 3x + 6$

15) 6

16) 14

17) 0

18) 2

19) 53

20) 2

21) 20

22) 11

23) 31

24) 73

25) 70

26) −45

27) 42

28) 15

29) 11

30) −16

31) 22

32) 22

33) 50

34) −3

35) 6

36) −11

37) −5

38) −21

39) 12

40) 31

41) 32

42) 18

43) 42

44) 1

45) 8

46) −3

47) −9

48) −5

49) −4

50) 8

51) 10

52) $\frac{1}{2}q - l = w$

53) $w = \frac{x}{2y}$

54) $T = \frac{PV}{nR}$

55) $d = a - b - c$

Solutions at bit.ly/3RAbyde

56) $(3, 2)$

57) $(3, 5)$

58) $(5, 3)$

59) $(4, 8)$

60) $(1, 3)$

61) $(3, -2)$

62) $(1, 4)$

63) $(1, 1)$

64) 4

65) 26

66) 5

67) 4

68) 13

69) 5

70) 17

71) 5

72) 34

73) 26

CHAPTER

8 Linear Functions

Math topics that you'll learn in this chapter:

☑ Finding Slope
☑ Writing Linear Equations
☑ Graphing Linear Inequalities
☑ Write an Equation from a Graph
☑ Slope-intercept Form and Point-slope Form
☑ Write a Point-slope Form Equation from a Graph
☑ Find $x-$ and $y-$intercepts in the Standard Form of Equation
☑ Graph an Equation in the Standard Form
☑ Equations of Horizontal and Vertical Lines
☑ Graph a Horizontal or Vertical line
☑ Graph an Equation in Point-Slope Form
☑ Equation of Parallel or Perpendicular Lines
☑ Compare Linear Function's Graph and Linear Equations
☑ Graphing Absolute Value Equations
☑ Two-variable Linear Equation Word Problems

Finding Slope

- The slope of a line represents the direction of a line on the coordinate plane.

- A coordinate plane contains two perpendicular number lines. The horizontal line is x and the vertical line is y. The point at which the two axes intersect is called the origin. An ordered pair (x, y) shows the location of a point.

- A line on a coordinate plane can be drawn by connecting two points.

- To find the slope of a line, we need the equation of the line or two points on the line.

- The slope of a line with two points $A(x_1, y_1)$ and $B(x_2, y_2)$ can be found by using this formula: $\frac{y_2 - y_1}{x_2 - x_1} = \frac{rise}{run}$.

- The equation of a line is typically written as $y = mx + b$ where m is the slope and b is the $y-$intercept.

Examples:

Example 1. Find the slope of the line through these two points:

$A(1, -6)$ and $B(3, 2)$.

Solution: Slope $= \frac{y_2 - y_1}{x_2 - x_1}$. Let (x_1, y_1) be $A(1, -6)$ and (x_2, y_2) be $B(3, 2)$.

(Remember, you can choose any point for (x_1, y_1) and (x_2, y_2)).

Then:
$$\text{Slope} = \frac{y_2 - y_1}{x_2 - x_1} = \frac{2 - (-6)}{3 - 1} = \frac{8}{2} = 4.$$

The slope of the line through these two points is 4.

Example 2. Find the slope of the line with equation $y = -2x + 8$.

Solution: When the equation of a line is written in the form of $y = mx + b$, the slope is m.

In this line: $y = -2x + 8$, the slope is -2.

bit.ly/3nMJYJv

Find more at

Writing Linear Equations

- The equation of a line in slope-intercept form: $y = mx + b$.

- To write the equation of a line, first identify the slope.

- Find the y −intercept. This can be done by substituting the slope and the coordinates of a point (x, y) on the line.

Examples:

Example 1. What is the equation of the line that passes through $(3, -4)$ and has a slope of 6?

Solution: The general slope-intercept form of the equation of a line is:
$$y = mx + b,$$
where m is the slope and b is the y −intercept.
By substitution of the given point and given slope:
$$y = mx + b \rightarrow -4 = (6)(3) + b.$$
So, $b = -4 - 18 = -22$, and the required equation of the line is: $y = 6x - 22$.

Example 2. Write the equation of the line through two points $A(3,1)$ and $B(-2,6)$.

Solution: First, find the slope: slope $= \frac{y_2 - y_1}{x_2 - x_1} = \frac{6-1}{-2-3} = \frac{5}{-5} = -1 \rightarrow m = -1$.
To find the value of b, use either point and plug in the values of x and y in the equation. The answer will be the same: $y = -x + b$. Let's check both points.
Then: $(3,1) \rightarrow y = mx + b \rightarrow 1 = -1(3) + b \rightarrow b = 4$.
$(-2,6) \rightarrow y = mx + b \rightarrow 6 = -1(-2) + b \rightarrow b = 4$.
The y −intercept of the line is 4. The equation of the line is: $y = -x + 4$.

Example 3. What is the equation of the line that passes through $(4, -1)$ and has a slope of 4?

Solution: The general slope-intercept form of the equation of a line is:
$$y = mx + b, \text{ where } m \text{ is the slope and } b \text{ is the } y \text{ −intercept.}$$
By substitution of the given point and given slope:
$$y = mx + b \rightarrow -1 = (4)(4) + b.$$
So, $b = -1 - 16 = -17$, and the equation of the line is: $y = 4x - 17$.

bit.ly/3nMKcAl

Find more at

Graphing Linear Inequalities

- To graph a linear inequality, first draw a graph of the "equals" line.

- Use a dashed line for less than (<) and greater than (>) signs and a solid line for less than and equal to ($\leq$) and greater than and equal to ($\geq$).

- Choose a testing point. (It can be any point on both sides of the line.)

- Put the value of (x, y) of that point in the inequality. If that works, that part of the line is the solution. If the values don't work, then the other part of the line is the solution.

Example:

Sketch the graph of inequality: $y < 2x + 4$.

Solution: To draw the graph of $y < 2x + 4$, you first need to graph the line:

$y = 2x + 4$.

Since there is a less than (<) sign, draw a dashed line.

The slope is 2 and the y −intercept is 4.

Then, choose a testing point and substitute the value of x and y from that point into the inequality. The easiest point to test is the origin: $(0,0)$.

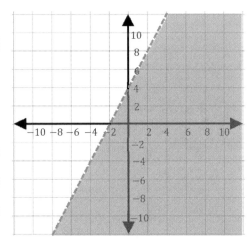

$(0,0) \rightarrow y < 2x + 4 \rightarrow 0 < 2(0) + 4 \rightarrow 0 < 4$.

This is correct! 0 is less than 4. So, this part of the line (on the right side) is the solution of this inequality.

Write an Equation from a Graph

- To write an equation of a line in slope-intercept form, given a graph of that equation, pick two points on the line and use them to find the slope. This is the value of m in the equation. Next, find the coordinates of the y−intercept these should be of the form $(0, b)$. The y−coordinate is the value of b in the equation.

- Finally, write the equation, substituting numerical values for m and b. Check your equation by picking a point on the line (Not the y−intercept) and plugging it in to see if it satisfies the equation.

Example:

Write the equation of the following line in slope-intercept form.

Solution: First, pick two points on the line

for example, $(2,1)$ and $(4,0)$.

Use these points to calculate the slope:

$$m = \frac{0-1}{4-2} = \frac{-1}{2} = -\frac{1}{2}.$$

Next, find the y−intercept:

$(0,2)$ Thus, $b = 2$.

Therefore, the equation of this line is:

$$y = -\frac{1}{2}x + 2.$$

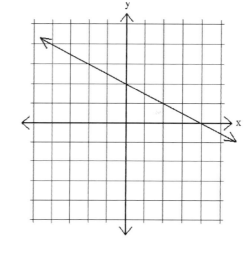

Now, let's check the equation by picking another point on the line. Let's choose

point $(-2,3)$.

Then:

$$(-2,3) \rightarrow y = -\frac{1}{2}x + 2 \rightarrow 3 = -\frac{1}{2}(-2) + 2 \rightarrow 3 = 1 + 2. \text{ This is true!}$$

bit.ly/3FDOsw1

Find more at

Slope-intercept Form and Point-slope Form

- The point-slope form of the equation of a straight line is: $y - y_1 = m(x - x_1)$. The equation is useful when we know: one point on the line: (x_1, y_1) and the slope of the line: m.

- The slope-intercept form is probably the most frequently used way to express the equation of a line. In general, the slope intercept form is:

$$y = mx + b$$

Examples:

Example 1. Find the equation of a line with point (1,5) and slope -3, and write it in slope-intercept and point-slope forms.

Solution: For point-slope form, we have the point and slope:

$$x_1 = 1, y_1 = 5, m = -3$$

Then: $y - y_1 = m(x - x_1) \rightarrow y - 5 = -3(x - 1)$

The slope-intercept form of a line is: $y = mx + b$

Since $y = 5, x = 1, m = -3$, we just need to solve for b

$$y = mx + b \rightarrow 5 = -3(1) + b \rightarrow b = 8$$

Slope-intercept form: $y = -3x + 8$

Example 2. Find the equation of a line with point (4,6) and slope 3, and write it in slope-intercept and point-slope forms.

Solution: For point-slope form, we have the point and slope:

$$x_1 = 4, y_1 = 6, m = 3$$

Then: $y - y_1 = m(x - x_1) \rightarrow y - 6 = 3(x - 4)$

The slope-intercept form of a line is: $y = mx + b$

Since $y = 6, x = 4, m = 3$, we just need to solve for b

$$y = mx + b \rightarrow 6 = 3(4) + b \rightarrow b = -6$$

Slope-intercept form: $y = 3x - 6$

Write a Point-slope Form Equation from a Graph

- The usage of the point-slope form equation is to determine the equation of a straight line when passes through a given point. In fact, you can use the point-slope formula only when you have the line's slope and a given point on the line. A line's equation with the slope of $'m'$ that passes through the point (x_1, y_1) can be found by the point-slope formula.

- The point-slope form equation is $y - y_1 = m(x - x_1)$. In this equation, (x_1, y_1) is considered as a random point on the line and m is a sign to represent the line's slope.

- To find the point-slope form equation of a straight line and solve it, you can follow the following steps:

  - 1st step: Find the slope, $'m'$ of the straight line. the slope formula is $m = \frac{change\ in\ y}{change\ in\ x}$. Then find the coordinates (x_1, y_1) of the random point on the line.
  - 2nd step: Put the values you found in the first step in the point-slope formula: $y - y_1 = m(x - x_1)$
  - 3rd step: Simplify the given equation to get the line's equation in the standard form.

Example:

According to the following graph, what is the equation of the line in point-slope form?

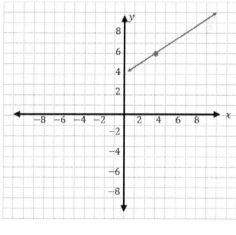

Solution: First, you should find the slope of the line (m). The coordinate of the red point is $(4,6)$. Consider another random point on the line such as $(7,8)$. Put this value in the slope formula: $m = \frac{change\ in\ y}{change\ in\ x} = \frac{8-6}{7-4} = \frac{2}{3} \rightarrow m = \frac{2}{3}$. Now write the equation in point-slope form using the coordinate of the red point is $(4,6)$ and $m = \frac{2}{3}$: $y - y_1 = m(x - x_1) \rightarrow y - 6 = \frac{2}{3}(x - 4)$. Therefore, the equation of the line in point-slope form is $y - 6 = \frac{2}{3}(x - 4)$.

Find $x-$ and $y-$intercepts in the Standard Form of Equation

- The linear equations' standard form (the general form) is described as $Ax + By = C$. In this form of the equation, $A, B,$ and C are integers, and the letters x and y are considered the variables.

- When you need to have a linear equation in the standard form, you can easily change it in a way that can be represented in the form $Ax + By = C$. Keep in mind that $A, B,$ and C should be integers and the order of the variables should be as mentioned in the standard form's equation.

- A line's $x-$intercept is the $x-$value when the line intersects the $x-$axis. In this case, y is equal to zero.

- A line's $y-$intercept is the $y-$value where the line intersects the $y-$axis. In this case, x is equal to zero.

Examples:

Example 1. Find the $x-$ and $y-$intercepts of line $6x + 24y = 12$.

Solution: To find the $x-$intercept, you can consider y equal to 0 and solve for $x: 6x + 24y = 12 \rightarrow 6x + 24(0) = 12 \rightarrow 6x = 12 \rightarrow x = 2$. The $x-$intercept is 2. To find the $y-$intercept, you can consider x equal to 0 and solve for $y: 6x + 24y = 12 \rightarrow 6(0) + 24y = 12 \rightarrow 24y = 12 \rightarrow y = \frac{1}{2}$. The $y-$intercept is $\frac{1}{2}$.

Example 2. Find the $x-$ and $y-$intercepts of line $3x + 5y = -15$.

Solution: To find the $x-$intercept, you can consider y equal to 0 and solve for $x: 3x + 5y = -15 \rightarrow 3x + 5(0) = -15 \rightarrow 3x = -15 \rightarrow x = -5$. The $x-$intercept is -5. To find the $y-$intercept, you can consider x equal to 0 and solve for $y: 3x + 5y = -15 \rightarrow 3(0) + 5y = -15 \rightarrow 5y = -15 \rightarrow y = -3$. The $y-$intercept is -3.

Example 3. Find the $x-$ and $y-$intercepts of line $-8x + 16y = 64$.

Solution: To find the $x-$intercept, you can consider y equal to 0 and solve for $x: -8x + 16y = 64 \rightarrow -8x + 16(0) = 64 \rightarrow -8x = 64 \rightarrow x = -8$. The $x-$intercept is -8. To find the $y-$intercept, you can consider x equal to 0 and solve for $y: -8x + 16y = 64 \rightarrow -8(0) + 16y = 64 \rightarrow 16y = 64 \rightarrow y = 4$. The $y-$intercept is 4.

Graph an Equation in the Standard Form

- The linear equations' standard form is $Ax + By = C$. In the standard form of the equation, the letters a, b, and c are all substituted with real numbers. The letter x refers to the independent variable and the letter y refers to the dependent variable.

- If an equation is expressed in standard form, then you can't find the slope and y-intercept that you need for graphing at first glance at the equation. In such a case, you must use a method to find these values.

- There are 2 different methods to graph a line in standard form. The first way is to convert the equation to slope-intercept form ($y = mx + b$) and then graph it. The second way is to find x and y−intercepts of the line in standard form and connect 2 intercepts and draw the line.

- The easiest way to graph an equation's line in standard form is by identifying intercepts. Keep in mind that at the y−intercept, the coordinate of x is equal to zero and that at the x-intercept, the coordinate of y is equal to zero. When you want to find the y−intercept, put x equal to zero and solve for y. When you want to find the x−intercept, set y equal to zero and solve for x. Then find the 2 intercepts on the coordinate plane and draw the line on the graph.

Example:

Graph the following equation: $6x - 4y = 24$

Solution: First, find the x−intercept. Consider $y = 0$ and solve for x: $6x - 4y = 24 \rightarrow 6x - 4(0) = 24 \rightarrow 6x = 24 \rightarrow x = 4$. The x−intercept is 4 and its coordinates are $(4,0)$. Now, find the y−intercept. Consider $x = 0$ and solve for y: $6x - 4y = 24 \rightarrow 6(0) - 4y = 24 \rightarrow -4y = 24 \rightarrow y = -6$. The y−intercept is -6 and its coordinates are $(0, -6)$.

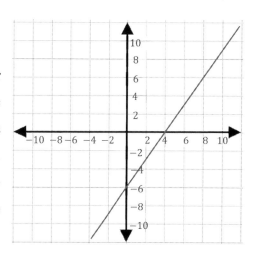

Now, find $(4,0)$ and $(0, -6)$ on the coordinate plane, and draw the line between these two points on the graph.

Equations of Horizontal and Vertical lines

- Horizontal lines have a slope of 0. Thus, in the slope-intercept equations $y = mx + b$, $m = 0$, the equation becomes $y = b$, where b is the y −coordinate of the y −intercept.

- Similarly, in the graph of a vertical line, x only takes one value. Thus, the equation for a vertical line is $x = a$, where a is the value that x takes.

Examples:

Example 1. Write an equation for the horizontal line that passes through $(6,2)$.

Solution: Since the line is horizontal, the equation of the line is in the form of:

$$y = b.$$

Where y always takes the same value of 2.

Thus, the equation of the line is:

$$y = 2.$$

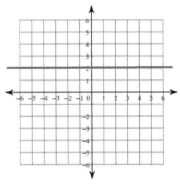

Example 2. Write an equation for the vertical line that passes through $(-3,5)$.

Solution: Since the line is vertical, the equation of the line is in the form of:

$$x = a.$$

Where x always takes the same value of -3.

Thus, the equation of the line is:

$$x = -3.$$

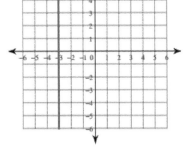

Graph a Horizontal or Vertical line

- When you graph a line, you usually need a point and the slope of the line to draw the line on the coordinate plane. But there are also exceptions that are called horizontal and vertical lines.

- The horizontal line is a kind of straight line that extends from left to right. An example of a horizontal line can be the x −axis. The horizontal line's slope is always zero because slope can be defined as "rise over run", and a horizontal line's rise is 0. Since the answer of dividing zero by any number is equal to zero, a horizontal line's slope always is zero. Horizontal lines are always parallel to the x −axis and they are written in the form $y = a$ where a is a real number.

- The vertical line is a kind of straight line that extends up and down. An example of a vertical line can be the y −axis. The vertical line's slope is always undefined because the run of a vertical line is zero. In fact, a number's quotient divided by zero is undefined, so a vertical line's slope is always undefined. Vertical lines are always parallel to the y −axis and they are written in the form $x = a$ where a is a real number.

Examples:

Example 1. Graph this equation: $y = -5$

Solution: $y = -5$ is a horizontal line and this equation tells you that every y −value is −5. You can consider some points that have a y −value of −5, then draw a line that connects the points.

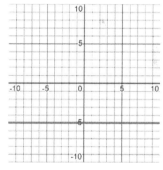

Example 2. Graph this equation: $x = 3$

Solution: $x = 3$ is a vertical line and this equation tells you that every x −value is 3. You can consider some points that have an x −value of 3, then draw a line that connects the points.

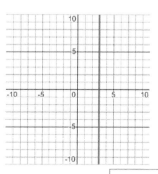

bit.ly/3D61ORj

Find more at

Graph an Equation in Point-Slope Form

- The point-slope form uses a slope and a point on a straight line to represent this line's equation. In fact, a line's equation with slope m that passes through the point (x_1, y_1) can be found by the point-slope form.

- The point-slope form's equation is $y - y_1 = m(x - x_1)$. In this equation, (x_1, y_1) is a point on the straight line and m is the line's slope.

- To graph an equation in point-slope form, follow these steps:

  - 1st step: First, check the point-slope form equation and be sure the equation uses subtraction the same as the point-slope form formula. If one side of the equation doesn't use subtraction operation, you should rewrite it with the subtraction sign.

  - 2nd step: Find a random point on the straight line and the slope of the line. The slope formula is $m = \frac{change\ in\ y}{change\ in\ x}$.

  - 3rd step: Use the random point and the value of the slope to graph the line.

Example:

Graph the following line: $y - 3 = -\frac{1}{3}(x + 5)$

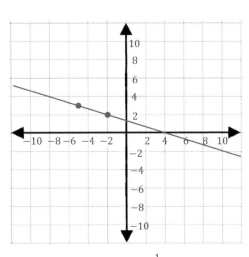

Solution: First, check the point-slope form equation. If one side of the equation doesn't use subtraction operation, you should rewrite it with the subtraction sign: $y - 3 = -\frac{1}{3}(x + 5) \rightarrow$ $y - 3 = -\frac{1}{3}(x - (-5))$. Find a random point on the straight line and the slope of the line. You can use the point that is used in the formula: $(x_1, y_1) \rightarrow (-5,3)$. The slope is $-\frac{1}{3}$. Use the random point and the value of slope to graph the line: find the point $(-5,3)$ on the coordinate plane. The slope is $-\frac{1}{3}$ and is the same as $\frac{-1}{3}$. So, move down 1 unit and right 3 units to find the other point on the straight line: $(-2,2)$. Connect these two points and graph the line.

Equation of Parallel and Perpendicular Lines

- Parallel lines have the same slope.

- Perpendicular lines have opposite-reciprocal slopes. If the slope of a line is m, its Perpendicular line has a slope of $-\frac{1}{m}$.

- Two lines are Perpendicular only if the product of their slopes is negative 1. $m_1 \times m_2 = -1$.

Examples:

Find the equation of a line that is:

Example 1. Parallel to $y = 2x + 1$ and passes through the point (5,4).

Solution: The slope of $y = 2x + 1$ is 2. We can solve it using the "point-slope" equation of a line: $y - y_1 = 2(x - x_1)$ and then put in the point (5,4):
$y - 4 = 2(x - 5)$.
You can also write it in slope-intercept format: $y = mx + b$.
$y - 4 = 2x - 10 \rightarrow y = 2x - 6$.

Example 2. Perpendicular to $y = -4x + 10$ and passes through the point (7,2).

Solution: The slope of $y = -4x + 10$ is -4. The negative reciprocal of that slope is: $m = \frac{-1}{-4} = \frac{1}{4}$. So, the perpendicular line has a slope of $\frac{1}{4}$.
Then: $y - y_1 = (\frac{1}{4})(x - x_1)$ and now put in the point (7,2): $y - 2 = (\frac{1}{4})(x - 7)$.
Slope-intercept $y = mx + b$ form: $y - 2 = \frac{x}{4} - \frac{7}{4} \rightarrow y = \frac{1}{4}x + \frac{1}{4}$

Example 3. Parallel to $y = 5x - 3$ and passes through the point $(4, -1)$.

Solution: The slope of $y = 5x - 3$ is 5. We can solve it using the "point-slope" equation of a line: $y - y_1 = 5(x - x_1)$ and then put in the point $(4, -1)$: $y - (-1) = 5(x - 4)$.
You can also write it in slope-intercept format: $y = mx + b$. $y + 1 = 5x - 20 \rightarrow y = 5x - 21$

Find more at
bit.ly/3ke2ieg

Compare Linear Function's Graph and Equations

- A linear function can be written in the form of $f(x) = mx + b$. In this form of equation m and b are real numbers.

- A linear graph provides a visual representation of a linear function and provides a straight line on the coordinate plane by connecting the points plotted on x and y coordinates.

- To compare a linear function's graph and linear equations, you should compare the slope or the $y-$intercept of them.

- To compare slopes of a linear function's graph and linear equations, find the change in y and the change in x between any 2 points on the graph's line. Then use the slope's equation ($m = \frac{change\ in\ y}{change\ in\ x}$) to find the value of m. After finding the value of m you can compare it with the value of m in a linear function.

- To compare the $y-$intercept of the linear function's graph and linear equations, you should first find the value of b in the graph. To determine $y-$intercept (b), see at which point the line crosses the $y-$axis. Then compare the $b-$value of the graph with the $b-$value of the linear function.

Example:

Compare the slope of function A and function B.

Function A　　　　Function B

$y = 2x - 6$

Solution: First, find the slope(m) of function A. Find the change in y and the change in x points $(2,0)$ and $(0,-6)$ on the line: $m = \frac{change\ in\ y}{change\ in\ x} : \frac{-6-0}{0-2} = 3$. Now, find the slope of function B. The equation of function B in the slope-intercept form is $y = 2x - 6$. Therefore, its slope is equal to 2. In the final step, compare the slopes.

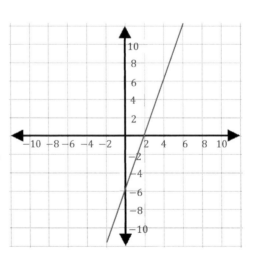

The slope of function A is 3 and is greater than the slope of function B (2).

Graphing Absolute Value Equations

- The general form of an absolute value function (that is linear) is:

$$y = |mx + b| + c$$

- The vertex (the lowest or the highest point) is located at $(\frac{-b}{m}, c)$.

- A vertical line that divides the graph into two equal halves is: $x = -\frac{b}{m}$.

- To graph an absolute value equation, find the vertex and some other points by substituting some values for x and solving for y.

Example:

Graph $y = |x + 2|$.

Solution: Find the vertex $(\frac{-b}{m}, c)$.

According to the general form of an absolute value function:

$$y = |mx + b| + c.$$

We have:

$$x = \frac{-b}{m} \rightarrow x = \frac{-2}{1} = -2.$$

And c is zero.

Then, the point $(-2, 0)$ is the vertex of the graph and represents the center of the table of

values. Create the table and plot the ordered pairs.

Now, find the points and graph the equation.

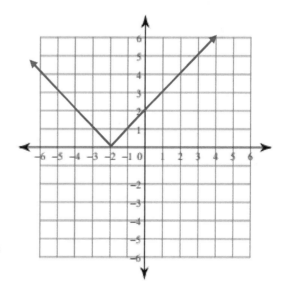

Two-variable Linear Equation Word Problems

- A two-variable linear equation is a kind of linear equation that has two variables with the exponent 1 and the solutions of can two-variable linear equation can be expressed in ordered pairs like (x, y).
- A two-variable linear equation can be seen in various forms like standard form, point-slope form, and slope-intercept form:
  - The standard form of a two-variable linear equation is $ax + by = c$. In this form of the equation, a, b, and c are real numbers and x and y are the variables.
  - The slope-intercept form of a two-variable linear equation is as $y = mx + b$. In this form of the equation, m is the line's slope and b is the y−intercept of the line.
  - The point-slope form of a two-variable linear equation is as $y - y_1 = m(x - x_1)$. In this form of the equation, (x_1, y_1) is a given point on the line and m is the line's slope.
- To write and solve a two-variable linear equation word problem you can follow these steps:
  - 1st step: Read the question carefully and ask yourself what is given information and what is needed in the question.
  - 2nd step: Determine the unknowns in the question and show them by x, and y variables.
  - 3rd step: Change the words of the problem to the mathematical language or math expression.
  - 4th step: Make a two-variable linear equation using the given information in the problem.
  - 5th step: In the last step, solve the equation to find the value of the unknowns.

Example:

John is going to buy a box of candies as a gift for his friend. He can add as many candies as he wants to this box at a price of \$3 per number. He also plans to buy a beautiful painting for \$20 as a gift. Show in an equation how the total cost, y, depends on the number of candies, x.

Solution: The cost of each candy = \$3 and the cost of the painting = \$20. Here, the number of candies is unknown, and we consider the variable x for it, and we show the total cost with the variable y. Therefore, our two-variable linear equation will be as follows:

$$y = 3x + 20.$$

Chapter 8: Practices

✎ Find the slope of each line.

1) $y = x - 5$

2) $y = 2x + 6$

3) $y = -5x - 8$

4) Line through $(2,6)$ and $(5,0)$

5) Line through $(8,0)$ and $(-4,3)$

6) Line through $(-2, -4)$ and $(-4,8)$

✎ Solve.

7) What is the equation of a line with slope 4 and intercept 16?

_____

8) What is the equation of a line with slope 3 and passes through point $(1,5)$? _____

9) What is the equation of a line with slope -5 and passes through point $(-2,7)$? _____

10) The slope of a line is -4 and it passes through point $(-6,2)$. What is the equation of the line? _____

11) The slope of a line is -3 and it passes through point $(-3, -6)$. What is the equation of the line? _____

✎ Sketch the graph of each linear inequality.

12) $y > 4x + 2$

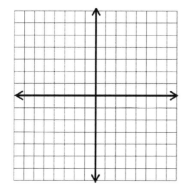

13) $y < -2x + 5$

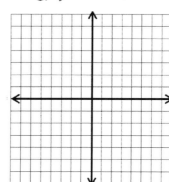

bit.ly/3RAbyde

Solutions at

✎ **Write an equation of each of the following line in slope-intercept from.**

14) _____

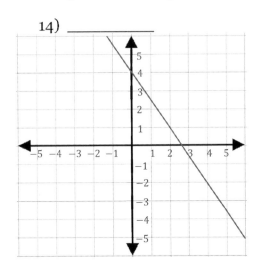

15) _____

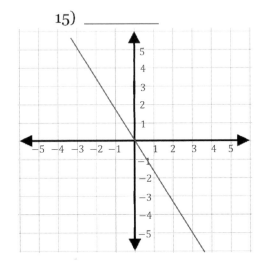

✎ **Find the equation of each line.**

16) Through: $(6, -6)$, slope $= -2$

Point-slope form: _____

Slope-intercept form: _____

17) Through: $(-7, 7)$, slope $= 4$

Point-slope form: _____

Slope-intercept form: _____

✎ **Write equation of the line in point-slope form.**

18)

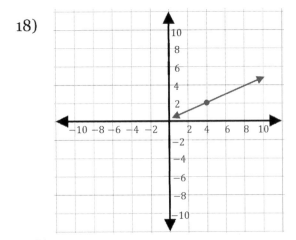

19)

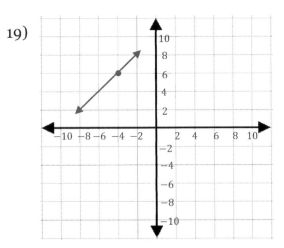

Find the x – intercept of each line.

20) $21x - 3y = -18$

21) $20x + 20y = -10$

22) $8x + 6y = 16$

23) $2x - 4y = -12$

Graph each equation.

24) $4x - 5y = 40$

25) $9x - 8y = -72$

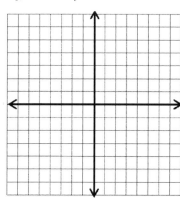 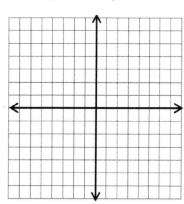

Find the equation of the following lines.

26) Write an equation for the horizontal line that passes through $(3, -5)$.

27) Write an equation for the horizontal line that passes through $(-4, 7)$.

28) Write an equation for the vertical line that passes through $(4, 0)$.

29) Write an equation for the vertical line that passes through $(0, -7)$.

Sketch the graph of each line.

30) Vertical line that passes through $(2, 6)$.

31) Horizontal line that passes through $(5, 3)$.

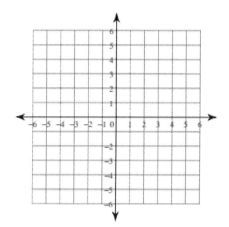 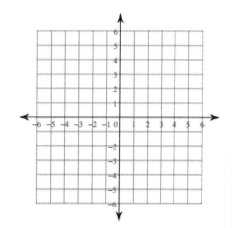

Solutions at bit.ly/3RAbyde

✍ **Graph each equation.**

32) $y + 3 = -\frac{1}{2}(x - 8)$

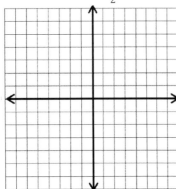

33) $y - 8 = -2(x - 1)$

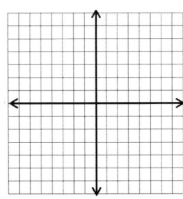

✍ **Find the equation of each line with the given information.**

34) Through: $(4, 4)$

Parallel to $y = -6x + 5$

Equation: _____

35) Through: $(7, 1)$

Perp. to $y = -\frac{1}{2}x - 4$

Equation: _____

36) Through: $(2, 0)$

Parallel to $y = x$

Equation: _____

37) Through: $(0, -4)$

Perp. to $y = 2x + 3$

Equation: _____

38) Through: $(-1, 1)$

Parallel to $y = 2$

Equation: _____

39) Through: $(3, 4)$

Perp. to $y = -x$

Equation: _____

✍ Compare the slope of the function *A* and function *B*.

40) Function *A*: 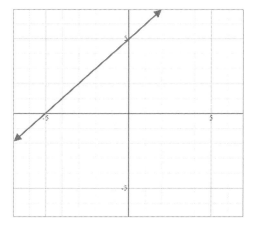 Function *B*: $y = 6x - 3$

41) Function *A*: 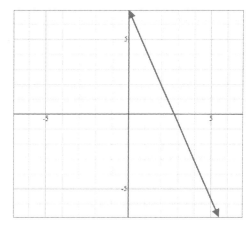 Function *B*: $y = -2.5x - 1$

42) Function *A*: 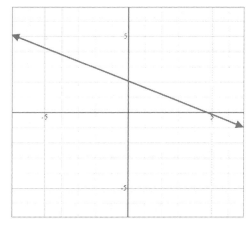 Function *B*: $y = 2x - 1$

✍ Graph each equation.

43) $y = -|x| - 1$

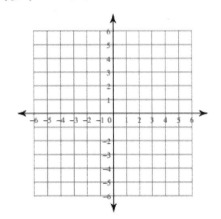

44) $y = -|x - 3|$

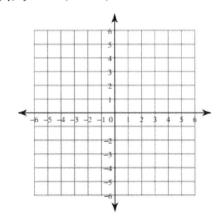

✍ Solve.

45) John has an automated hummingbird feeder. He fills it to capacity, 8 fluid ounces. It releases 1 fluid ounce of nectar every day. Write an equation that shows how the number of fluid ounces of nectar left, y, depends on the number of days John has filled it, x.

46) The entrance fee to Park City is $9. Additionally, skate rentals cost $4 per hour. Write an equation that shows how the total cost, y, depends on the length of the rental in hours, x.

Chapter 8: Answers

1) 1
2) 2
3) -5
4) -2
5) $-\frac{1}{4}$

6) -6
7) $y = 4x + 16$
8) $y = 3x + 2$
9) $y = -5x - 3$
10) $y = -4x - 22$
11) $y = -3x - 15$

12) $y > 4x + 2$

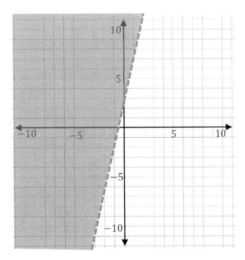

13) $y < -2x + 5$

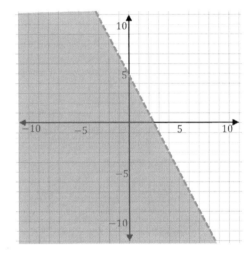

14) $y = -\frac{3}{2}x + 4$

15) $y = -\frac{5}{3}x$

16) Point-slope form: $y + 6 = -2(x - 6)$

Slope-intercept form: $y = -2x + 6$

17) Point-slope form: $y - 7 = 4(x + 7)$

Slope-intercept form: $y = 4x + 35$

18) $(y - 2) = \frac{1}{2}(x - 4)$

19) $(y - 6) = (x + 4)$

20) $-\frac{6}{7}$

21) $-\frac{1}{2}$

22) 2

23) -6

bit.ly/3RAbyde

Solutions at

24)

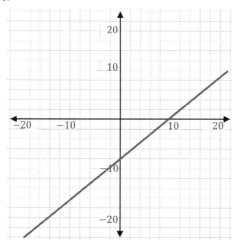

25)

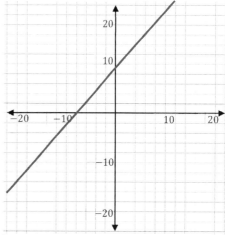

26) $y = -5$

27) $y = 7$

28) $x = 4$

29) $x = 0$

30)

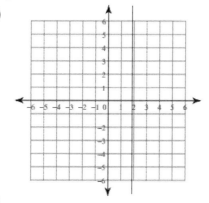

31)

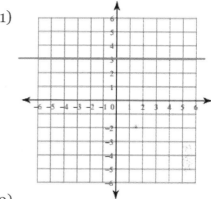

32)

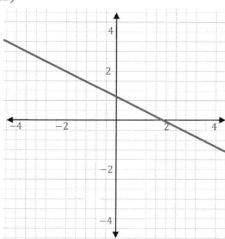

33)

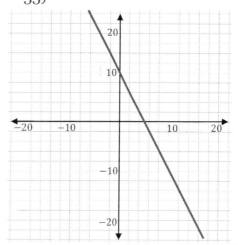

Solutions at

34) $y = -6x + 28$

35) $y = 2x - 13$

36) $y = x - 2$

37) $y = -\frac{1}{2}x - 4$

38) $y = 1$

39) $y = x + 1$

40) The slope of function A is 1 and is lower that than the slope of function B (6).

41) Two functions are parallel.

42) Two functions are intersecting.

43) $y = -|x| - 1$

44) $y = -|x - 3|$

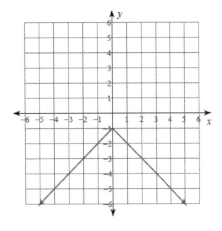

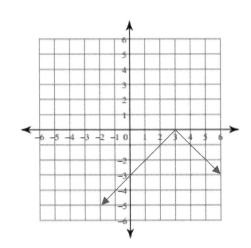

45) $y = -x + 8$

46) $y = 4x + 9$

9 Inequalities and System of Equations

Math topics that you'll learn in this chapter:

- ☑ One–Step Inequalities
- ☑ Multi–Step Inequalities
- ☑ Compound Inequalities
- ☑ Write a Linear Inequality from a Graph
- ☑ Graph Solutions to Linear Inequalities
- ☑ Solve Advanced Linear Inequalities in Two-Variables
- ☑ Graph Solutions to Advanced Linear Inequalities
- ☑ Absolute Value Inequalities
- ☑ Systems of Equations
- ☑ Find the Number of Solutions to a Linear Equation
- ☑ Write a System of Equations Given a Graph
- ☑ Systems of Equations Word Problems
- ☑ Solve Linear Equations Word Problems
- ☑ Systems of Linear Inequalities
- ☑ Write Two-variable Inequalities Word Problems

One–Step Inequalities

- An inequality compares two expressions using an inequality sign. Inequality signs are: "less than" <, "greater than" >, "less than or equal to" ≤, and "greater than or equal to" ≥.

- You only need to perform one Math operation to solve the one-step inequalities.

- To solve one-step inequalities, find the inverse (opposite) operation is being performed. For dividing or multiplying both sides by negative numbers, flip the direction of the inequality sign.

- You can use "interval notation" to write the answers to inequalities. Interval notation is a way of representing the solutions of an inequality. Brackets and parentheses are used to indicate if the endpoints are included or excluded from the solution set. For example, consider the inequality $x > 2$. The solution set for this inequality is all real numbers greater than 2, extending to infinity. The interval notation for this solution set would be $(2, \infty)$, meaning that x is any number greater than 2 but does not include 2.

- If the inequality is $x \geq 2$, the solution set would include 2, and the interval notation for this solution set would be $[2, \infty)$, meaning that x is any number greater than or equal to 2, including 2. Keep in mind that we also have negative infinity that is represented by the symbol "$-\infty$".

Examples:

Example 1. Solve this inequality for x. $x + 5 \geq 4$

Solution: The inverse (opposite) operation of addition is subtraction. In this inequality, 5 is added to x. To isolate x we need to subtract 5 from both sides of the inequality.
Then: $x + 5 \geq 4 \rightarrow x + 5 - 5 \geq 4 - 5 \rightarrow x \geq -1$.
The solution is: $x \geq -1$ or $[-1, \infty)$

Example 2. Solve the inequality. $x - 3 > -6$

Solution: 3 is subtracted from x. Add 3 to both sides.
$x - 3 > -6 \rightarrow x - 3 + 3 > -6 + 3 \rightarrow x > -3$ or $[-3, \infty)$

Multi−Step Inequalities

- To solve a multi-step inequality, combine "like" terms on one side.

- Bring variables to one side by adding or subtracting.

- Isolate the variable.

- Simplify using the inverse of addition or subtraction.

- Simplify further by using the inverse of multiplication or division.

- For dividing or multiplying both sides by negative numbers, flip the direction of the inequality sign.

Examples:

Example 1. Solve this inequality. $8x - 2 \leq 14$

Solution: In this inequality, 2 is subtracted from $8x$. The inverse of subtraction is addition. Add 2 to both sides of the inequality:

$$8x - 2 + 2 \leq 14 + 2 \rightarrow 8x \leq 16.$$

Now, divide both sides by 8. Then:

$$8x \leq 16 \rightarrow \frac{8x}{8} \leq \frac{16}{8} \rightarrow x \leq 2.$$

The solution of this inequality is $x \leq 2$ or $(-\infty, 2]$

Example 2. Solve this inequality. $3x + 9 < 12$

Solution: First, subtract 9 from both sides: $3x + 9 - 9 < 12 - 9$.
Then simplify:

$$3x + 9 - 9 < 12 - 9 \rightarrow 3x < 3.$$

Now divide both sides by 3: $\frac{3x}{3} < \frac{3}{3} \rightarrow x < 1$ or $(-\infty, 1)$

Example 3. Solve this inequality. $-5x + 3 \geq 8$

Solution: First, subtract 3 from both sides:

$$-5x + 3 - 3 \geq 8 - 3 \rightarrow -5x \geq 5.$$

Divide both sides by -5. Remember that you need to flip the direction of inequality sign.

$$-5x \geq 5 \rightarrow \frac{-5x}{-5} \leq \frac{5}{-5} \rightarrow x \leq -1 \text{ or } (-\infty, -1]$$

Compound Inequalities

- A compound inequality includes two or more inequalities that are separated by the words "and" or "or".

- To solve compound inequalities, isolate the variable, flip the sign for negative division, and simplify using inverse operations.

- To solve compound inequality with the word "and," you must look for numbers that are solutions for all inequalities or the intersection of the inequalities.

- To solve a compound inequality with the word "or", first solve each inequality. Then graph the solutions. To find the solution to the compound inequality, we look at the graphs of each inequality, find the numbers that belong to each graph and put all those numbers together.

- To combine the solution sets of two or more inequalities, use union symbol "∪". For example, consider the inequalities $x < -5$ and $x > 2$. The solution sets for these inequalities can be represented as $(-\infty, -5)$ and $(2, \infty)$ respectively in interval notation. The union of these two intervals represents the combined solution set $x < -5$ or $x > 2$, which is $(-\infty, -5) \cup (2, \infty)$.

Examples:

Example 1. Solve. $6 < 3x \leq 24$

Solution: To solve this inequality, divide all sides of the inequality by 3. This simplifies the inequality as follows: $2 < x \leq 8$ or $(2, 8]$.

Example 2. Solve. $x - 5 < -9$ or $\frac{x}{5} > 3$

Solution: Solve each inequality by isolating the variable:
$x - 5 < -9 \rightarrow x - 5 + 5 < -9 + 5 \rightarrow x < -4$.
Then:
$\frac{x}{5} > 3 \rightarrow \frac{x}{5} \times 5 > 3 \times 5 \rightarrow x > 15$.

The solution to these two inequalities is:
$x < -4$ or $x > 15$ or $(-\infty, -4) \cup (15, \infty)$

Write a Linear Inequality from a Graph

- When 2 linear expressions are compared by the inequality symbols ($<, >, \leq,$) they make linear inequalities.
- The graph of inequality is represented by a dashed line or solid line, and one shaded side. With clues from a linear inequality graph and your information about linear relationships, you can find the equation of linear inequality.
- To write a linear inequality from a graph, follow these steps:
  - 1st step: Look at the graph and determine whether the inequality line is a dashed line or a solid line. If it's a dashed line, the sign of inequality is $<$ or $>$. If it's a solid line, the sign of inequality is $\leq$ or $\geq$.
  - 2nd step: Consider 2 points on the inequality line. Using these two points you can determine the equation of the inequality.
  - 3rd step: Find the inequality line's slope by these two points. To find slope you can use the slope's formula: $m = \frac{(y_2 - y_1)}{(x_2 - x_1)}$
  - 4th step: Put the value of slope and a point into the formula $y = mx + b$. In this formula, m is the slope of the line and (x, y) is a point on the line and the value of b is the y-intercept.
  - 5th step: Look at the graph's shaded part and determine whether y is less than the obtained equation or greater than the obtained equation. You can put a point from the shaded part into the equation to find the sign of inequality.

Example:

Write the slope-intercept form equation of the following graph.

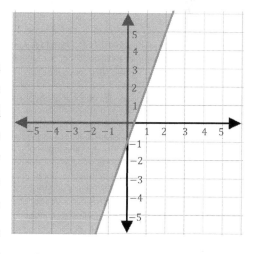

Solution: To write the inequality equation in slope-intercept form, you should find the y−intercept (b), and the slope (m), of the solid line. The value of b is -1 because the solid line passes through the y−axis at $(0, -1)$. Now consider 2 points on the solid line to find the slope. You can use $(0, -1)$ and $(-1, -4)$: $m = \frac{(y_2 - y_1)}{(x_2 - x_1)} = \frac{-4 + 1}{-1 - 0} = \frac{-3}{-1} = 3 \rightarrow m = 3$. Now use the value of b and m and put them into the slope-intercept form formula: $y = mx + b \rightarrow y = 3x - 1$. Determine the symbol of inequality: you have a solid line, and the shaded part is above the line. So, the equation of the inequality is as follows: $y \geq 3x - 1$.

Find more at
bit.ly/3IOHne0

Graph Solutions to Linear Inequalities

- A math statement that compares 2 expressions by an inequality sign is called an inequality. In inequalities, an inequality's expression can be greater or less than the other expression. The special sign should be used in inequalities $(\leq, \geq, >, <)$.
- Inequalities that you can solve using only one step are called one-step inequalities. Inequalities that you should take two steps to solve are called two-step inequalities.
- To solve one-step and two-step linear inequalities for a variable, you should use inverse operations to undo the operations and isolate the variable in the inequality. Remember you should do the same operation for two sides of the inequality. Reverse the inequality symbol's direction when you multiply or divide by a negative number.
- To graph an inequality, include a number using a filled-in circle and exclude a number using an open circle.

Examples:

Example 1. Solve the following inequality and graph the solution.

$$m + 3 \geq 8$$

Solution: Solve for m: $m + 3 \geq 8 \rightarrow m \geq 8 - 3 \rightarrow m \geq 5$. Now graph $m \geq 5$. The inequality $m \geq 5$ means that m can be any number more than or equal to 5. m can be equal to 5, so you should use a filled-in circle located on 5. Also, m can be more than 5, so you should also draw an arrow pointing to the right:

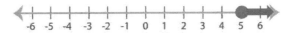

Example 2. Solve the following inequality and graph the solution.

$$-5q - 3 < 7$$

Solution: $-5q - 3 < 7$ is a two-step inequality. First, solve for q: $-5q - 3 < 7 \rightarrow -5q < 3 + 7 \rightarrow -5q < 10 \rightarrow q > -2$. Now graph $q > -2$. The inequality $q > -2$ means that q can be any number more than -2. q can't be equal to -2, so you should use an open circle located on -2. Also, q can be more than -2, so you should also draw an arrow pointing to the right:

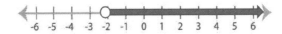

Solve Advanced Linear Inequalities in Two-Variables

- The general form of a linear inequality in two-variable is as

  $$Ax + By < C,$$

  Where the sign less than ($<$) can be any of greater than ($>$), less than and equal to ($\leq$), greater than and equal to ($\geq$), or not equal to ($\neq$).

- To solve a linear inequality, convert the given inequality to the general form.

- Use the inverse operations to undo the inequality operations for both sides of the inequality to arrive at the general form.

- To solve a linear inequality in two-variable in general form all ordered pairs like (x, y) produce a true statement when the values of x and y are substituted into the inequality.

Examples:

Example 1. Solve the inequality $3x - 2 \geq 4y + x$.

Solution: First, convert to the general form. Add 2 to both sides of the inequality. So,

$$3x - 2 + 2 \geq 4y + x + 2 \rightarrow 3x \geq 4y + x + 2.$$

Subtract $4y$ from both sides as $3x - 4y \geq 4y + x + 2 - 4y \rightarrow 3x - 4y \geq x + 2$.

Also, subtract x from the sides:

$$3x - 4y \geq x + 2 \rightarrow 3x - 4y - x \geq x + 2 - x \rightarrow 2x - 4y \geq 2.$$

The answer to this inequality is all ordered pairs in the form of (x, y) where $y \leq \frac{x-1}{2}$. That is, $\left\{ (x, y) | x \in \mathbb{R}, y \leq \frac{x-1}{2} \right\}$.

Example 2. Solve the inequality $y + 3 < x + 1$.

Solution: Convert to the general form. Subtract 1 from both sides. So,

$$y + 3 - 1 \geq x + 1 - 1 \rightarrow y + 2 < x.$$

Now, subtract y from both sides $y + 2 < x \rightarrow x - y > 2$. The answer to this inequality is all ordered pairs in the form of (x, y) where $x > y + 2$. That is, $\{ (x, y) | y \in R, x > y + 2 \}$.

Graph Solutions to Advanced Linear Inequalities

- Use the inverse operations to undo the inequality operations for both sides of the inequality.

- For dividing or multiplying both sides by negative numbers, flip the direction of the inequality sign.

- Continue simplifying until the variable is on one side of the inequality and the other components on the other side.

- To graph an inequality, use a filled-in circle to represent a number and an open circle to remove the number from the graph.

Examples:

Example 1. Solve the inequality $3x + 1 \geq 3 - x$.

Solution: Subtract 1 from both sides $3x + 1 - 1 \geq 3 - x - 1 \rightarrow 3x \geq 2 - x$. Now, add x to the sides of the obtained inequality. So, $3x + x \geq 2 - x + x \rightarrow 4x \geq 2$. Finally, divide by 4 and simplify. Therefore, $4x \geq 2 \rightarrow x \geq \frac{1}{2}$.

To graph, put a filled-in circle instead of the point $\frac{1}{2}$ on the real number axis and draw a line to positive infinity. As follow:

Example 2. Solve the inequality $\frac{x+3}{-3} < 2x + 1$.

Solution: Multiply -3 by both sides and since -3 is a negative number, then flip the direction of the inequality sign. So, $-3\left(\frac{x+3}{-3}\right) > -3(2x + 1) \rightarrow x + 3 > -6x - 3$. Add $6x$ to the sides of the inequalities: $x + 3 + 6x > -6x - 3 + 6x \rightarrow 7x + 3 > -3$. Now, subtract 3, $7x + 3 - 3 > -3 - 3 \rightarrow 7x > -6$. Finally, divide both sides of the inequality by 7. Therefore, $7x > -6 \rightarrow x > -\frac{6}{7}$. To graph, put an open circle instead of the point $-\frac{6}{7}$ on the axis and draw a line to $+\infty$. We have:

Absolute Value Inequalities

- An absolute value inequality includes an absolute value $|a|$ and a sign of inequality $(<, >, \leq, \geq)$.

- To solve an absolute value inequality, change it from an absolute value to a simple inequality.

- The method of transforming absolute value inequality into simple inequality depends on the direction that the inequality refers to. Depending on the direction of the inequality, use one of the following methods:

  ❖ To solve x in the inequality $|ax + b| < c$, you must solve

  $-c < ax + b < c$.

  ❖ To solve x in the inequality $|ax + b| > c$ you must solve $ax + b > c$ and

  $ax + b < -c$.

Examples:

Example 1. Solve. $|2x - 1| \leq 5$.

Solution: Since the inequality sign is $\leq$, rewrite the inequality to:

$$-5 \leq 2x - 1 \leq 5.$$

Then, solve the inequality:

$$-5 \leq 2x - 1 \leq 5 \rightarrow -4 \leq 2x \leq 6$$

Now, divide each section by 2:

$$-4 \leq 2x \leq 6 \rightarrow \frac{-4}{2} \leq \frac{2x}{2} \leq \frac{6}{2} \rightarrow -2 \leq x \leq 3$$

You can also write this solution using the interval symbol: $[-2, 3]$

Example 2. Solve. $|x + 3| > 11$.

Solution: Since the inequality sign is $>$, rewrite the inequality to:

$$x + 3 > 11 \text{ or } x + 3 < -11.$$

Now, simplify both inequalities:

$x + 3 > 11 \rightarrow x > 8 \text{ or } x + 3 < -11 \rightarrow x < -14 \text{ or } (-\infty, -14) \cup (8, +\infty)$

bit.ly/3LbbqfV
Find more at

System of Equations

- A system of equations contains two equations and two variables. For example, consider the system of equations: $x - y = 1$, $x + y = 5$.

- The easiest way to solve a system of equations is by the elimination method. The elimination method uses the addition property of equality. You can add the same value to each side of an equation.

- For the first equation above, you can add $x + y$ to the left side and 5 to the right side of the first equation: $x - y + (x + y) = 1 + 5$. Now, if you simplify, you get: $x - y + (x + y) = 1 + 5 \rightarrow 2x = 6 \rightarrow x = 3$. Now, substitute 3 for the x in the first equation: $3 - y = 1$. By solving this equation, $y = 2$.

Examples:

Example 1. What is the value of $x + y$ in this system of equations? $\begin{cases} x + 2y = 6 \\ 2x - y = -8 \end{cases}$

Solution: Solving a System of Equations by Elimination: multiply the first equation by (-2), then add it to the second equation.

$$\begin{matrix} -2(x + 2y = 6) \\ \underline{2x - y = -8} \end{matrix} \rightarrow \begin{matrix} -2x - 4y = -12 \\ 2x - y = -8 \end{matrix} \rightarrow -5y = -20 \rightarrow y = 4$$

Plug in the value of y into one of the equations and solve for x.
$$x + 2(4) = 6 \rightarrow x + 8 = 6 \rightarrow x = 6 - 8 \rightarrow x = -2.$$
Thus,
$$x + y = -2 + 4 = 2.$$

Example 2. What is the value of $y - x$ in this system of equations? $\begin{cases} -x + 3y = 2 \\ 3x - y = -2 \end{cases}$

Solution: Solving a System of Equations by Elimination: multiply the second equation by (3), then add it to the first equation.

$$\begin{matrix} -x + 3y = 2 \\ 3(3x - y = -2) \end{matrix} \rightarrow \begin{matrix} -x + 3y = 2 \\ 9x - 3y = -6 \end{matrix} \rightarrow 8x = -4 \rightarrow x = -\frac{1}{2}.$$

Plug in the value of y into one of the equations and solve for y.

$$-\left(-\frac{1}{2}\right) + 3y = 2 \rightarrow \frac{1}{2} + 3y = 2 \rightarrow 3y = \frac{3}{2} \rightarrow y = \frac{1}{2}.$$

Thus, $y - x = \frac{1}{2} - \left(-\frac{1}{2}\right) = \frac{1}{2} + \frac{1}{2} = 1.$

Find the Number of Solutions to a Linear Equation

- The linear equation is a kind of equation with the highest degree of 1. In other words, in a linear equation, there is no variable with an exponent more than 1. A linear equation's graph always is in the form of a straight line, it's called a 'linear equation'.

- The linear equation has no solution if by solving a linear equation you get a false statement as an answer.

- The linear equation has one solution if by solving a linear equation you get a true statement for a single value for the variable.

- The equation has infinitely many solutions if by solving a linear equation you get a statement that is always true.

Examples:

Example 1. How many solutions does the following equation have?

$$7 - 4p = -4p$$

Solution: Solve for p: $7 - 4p = -4p \rightarrow 7 = +4p - 4p \rightarrow 7 = 0$. $7 = 0$ is a false statement. The linear equation has no solution because by solving the linear equation you get a false statement as an answer.

Example 2. How many solutions does the following equation have?

$$12h = 3h + 27$$

Solution: Solve for h: $12h = 3h + 27 \rightarrow 12h - 3h = 27 \rightarrow 9h = 27 \rightarrow h = 3$. $h = 3$ is a true statement for a single value for the variable. So, the linear equation has one solution because by solving a linear equation you get a true statement for a single value for the variable.

Example 3. How many solutions does the following equation have?

$$8n - 2n = 6n$$

Solution: Simplify the left side of the equation
$8n - 2n = 6n \rightarrow 6n = 6n$. $6n = 6n$ is a statement that is always true. So, the equation has infinitely many solutions because by solving a linear equation you get a statement that is always true.

bit.ly/3iWpa57

Find more at

Write a System of Equations Given a Graph

- A system of equations consists of 2 or more equations and tries to find common solutions to the equations. In fact, a system of linear equations is an equation set in which the same set of variables can satisfy it."

- To write a system of equations given a graph, first, you should know each line in the graph shows a linear equation, and the two equations make a system of equations.

- Look at the first line. To write its equation, find the slope (m), and $y-$intercept (b). To find the slope, you can use any two points on the line and plug the, in the slope equation: $m = \frac{change\ in\ y}{change\ in\ x}$. To determine $y-$intercept (b), see at which point the line crosses the $y-$axis. Then use the value of slope and $y-$intercept to construct the line's equation in slope-intercept form. You can find the second line's equation in the same way.

Example:

Write a system of equations for the following graph.

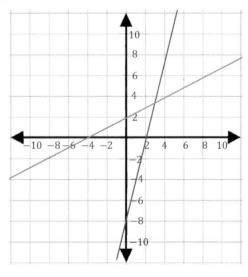

Solution: First, look at the green line. write its equation by identifying the slope (m) and $y-$intercept (b): to find the slope, you can use any two points on the line and plug in the slope equation: $m = \frac{change\ in\ y}{change\ in\ x}$.

Here choose the points $(0,2)$ and $(-4,0)$: $\frac{0-2}{-4-0} = \frac{1}{2}$. The green line crosses the $y-$axis at $(0,2)$, so the $y-$intercept is $b = 2$. Now write the equation of the green line: $y = \frac{1}{2}x + 2$. You can find the red line's equation in the same way. Use the points $(0,-8)$ and $(2,0)$: $\frac{0+8}{2-0} = 4$. The red line crosses the $y-$axis at $(0,-8)$, so the $y-$intercept is $b = -8$. Now write the equation of the red line: $y = 4x - 8$. Therefore, the graph shows the following system of equations:$\begin{cases} y = \frac{1}{2}x + 2 \\ y = 4x - 8 \end{cases}$

Systems of Equations Word Problems

To solve systems of equations word problems:

- Find the key information in the problem that will help write two equations.

- Define two variables x and y.

- Write two equations using the variables.

- Choose a method (elimination, substitution, etc.) for solving the system of equations.

- Check your answers by substituting solutions into the original equations.

- Answer the questions in the real-world problems.

Example:

Tickets to a movie cost $8 for adults and $5 for students. A group of friends purchased 20 tickets for $115. How many adult tickets did they buy?

Solution: Let x be the number of adult tickets and y be the number of student tickets. There are 20 tickets.

Then: $x + y = 20$. The cost of adults' tickets is $8 and for students' it is $5, and the total cost is $115. So, $8x + 5y = 115$. Now, we have a system of equations:

$$\begin{cases} x + y = 20 \\ 8x + 5y = 115 \end{cases}.$$

To solve this system of equations, multiply the first equation by -5 and add it to the second equation: $-5(x + y = 20) = -5x - 5y = -100$.

$8x + 5y + (-5x - 5y) = 115 - 100 \rightarrow 3x = 15 \rightarrow x = 5 \rightarrow 5 + y = 20 \rightarrow y = 15$.

There are 5 adult tickets and 15 student tickets. Now, check your answers by substituting solutions into the original equations.

$x + y = 20 \rightarrow 5 + 15 = 20, \; 8x + 5y = 115 \rightarrow 8(5) + 5(15) = 115 \rightarrow 40 + 75 = 115$.

The solutions are correct in both equations.

bit.ly/3koWCP3

Find more at

Solve Linear Equations' Word Problems

- A linear equation in one variable that you can solve in only one step is called a one-step equation.

- A linear equation in one variable that you should take two steps to solve is called a two-step equation.

- To solve word problems involving one-step and two-step linear equations, you can follow these steps:

  - 1st step: Read the whole problem carefully and determine what you are asked to find.

  - 2nd step: Look for keywords and put variables for the unknown amount.

  - 3rd step: Use the information you find and write an algebraic equation.

  - 4th step: Solve the equation. You should isolate the variable in your linear equation. Use simple math operations to isolate the variable. Remember when you use an operation for one side of the equation, you must also do the same for the other side. Once you've solved the linear equation, you've got the variable's value that makes the linear equation true.

Example:

Larry is in a chocolate shop and is going to buy some chocolates for his friends. He chooses 4 chocolates with a flower design and in addition, he also chooses some packs of three chocolates. If the total number of chocolates he has bought is 28, write an equation that you can use to find p, the number of packs of three chocolates. How many packs of three chocolates has Larry bought?

Solution: Larry chooses some packs of three chocolates and m is the number of packs of three chocolates. We can write it as follows: $3p$. He also chooses 4 chocolates with a flower design. The total number of chocolates he has bought is 28. Therefore, we can complete the equation as follows: $3p + 4 = 28$. The equation $3p + 4 = 28$ can be used to find how many packs of three chocolates Larry bought. Solve the equation for $p: 3p + 4 = 28 \rightarrow 3p = 28 - 4 \rightarrow 3p \rightarrow 24 \rightarrow p = 24 \div 3 = 8 \rightarrow p = 8$. So, he bought 8 packs of three chocolates.

Systems of Linear Inequalities

- A system of linear inequalities is a set of two or more inequalities. Each of the inequalities is solved separately, and the common answer between these inequalities is the answer of the linear inequality system.

- If you cannot mentally find the answers to the inequalities, just draw on their axis and find the common ground.

Example:

Solve the following system of inequalities:

$$\begin{cases} 8x - 4y \leq 12 \\ 3x + 6y \leq 12 \\ \quad y \geq 0 \end{cases}$$

Solution: As much as possible, we simplify each of the inequalities based on y:

$$\begin{cases} 8x - 4y \leq 12 \rightarrow -4y \leq -8x + 12 \rightarrow y \geq 2x - 3 \\ 3x + 6y \leq 12 \rightarrow 6y \leq -3x + 12 \rightarrow y \leq -\dfrac{x}{2} + 2 \\ \qquad\qquad\qquad\qquad y \geq 0 \end{cases} \rightarrow \begin{cases} y \geq 2x - 3 \\ y \leq -\dfrac{x}{2} + 2 \\ y \geq 0 \end{cases}$$

Draw a graph for each inequality. The answer to the system of inequalities is the common points between the graphs:

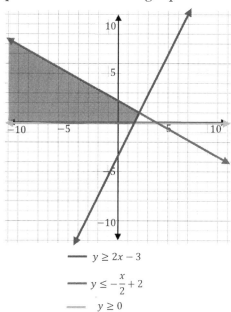

— $y \geq 2x - 3$

— $y \leq -\dfrac{x}{2} + 2$

— $y \geq 0$

Write Two-variable Inequalities Word Problems

- The two-variable linear inequalities describe a not equal relationship between 2 algebraic statements that contain two different variables. A two-variables linear inequality is created when two variables are involved in the equation and inequality symbols ($<, >, \leq,$ or $\geq$) are used to connect 2 algebraic expressions.

- The two-variables linear inequalities' solution can be expressed as an ordered pair (x, y). When the x and y values of the ordered pair are replaced in the inequality they make a correct expression.

- The method of solving a linear inequality is like the method of solving a linear equation. The difference between these two methods is in the symbol of inequality. You solve linear inequalities' word problems in the same way as linear equations' word problems:

  - 1st step: First, read the problem and try to write an inequality in words in a way that expresses the situation well.
  - 2nd step: Represent each of the given information with numbers, symbols, and variables.
  - 3rd step: Compare the inequality you've written in words with the given information that you've represented with numbers, symbols, and variables. Then rewrite what you've found out in the form of an inequality expression.
  - 4th step: Simplify both sides of the inequality. Once you find the values, you have one of these inequalities:
    - Strict inequalities: In this case, both sides of the inequalities can't be equal to each other.
    - Non-strict inequalities: In this case, both sides of the inequalities can be equal.

Example:

Sara plans to hold a party. She plans to order pizza and pasta from a restaurant for dinner. The cost of each pizza is $45 and the cost of each pasta is $30. She hopes to spend no more than $400 on dinner. Write a linear inequality so that x represents the number of pizzas and y represents the number of pasta.

Solution: First, try to write an inequality in words in a way that expresses the situation well: The cost of the pizzas plus the cost of the pasta is no more than $400. Now, represent each of the given information with numbers, symbols, and variables: The cost of the pizzas is $45 times the number of pizzas, which is x. The product is $45x$. The cost of the pasta is $30 times the number of pasta, which is y. The product is $30y$. No more than means less than or equal ($\leq$). Rewrite what you've found out in the form of an inequality expression: $45x + 30y \leq 400$.

Chapter 9: Practices

✍ Solve each inequality and graph it.

1) $x - 2 \geq -2$

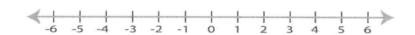

2) $2x - 3 < 9$

✍ Solve each inequality.

3) $x + 13 > 4$

4) $x + 6 > 5$

5) $-12 + 2x \leq 26$

6) $-2 + 8x \leq 14$

7) $6 + 4x \leq 18$

8) $4(x + 3) \geq -12$

9) $2(6 + x) \geq -12$

10) $3(x - 5) < -6$

11) $10 + 5x < -15$

12) $6(6 + x) \geq -18$

13) $2(x - 5) \geq -14$

14) $6(x + 4) < -12$

15) $3(x - 8) \geq -48$

16) $-(6 - 4x) > -30$

17) $2(2 + 2x) > -60$

18) $-3(4 + 2x) > -24$

✍ Solve each inequality.

19) $5x \leq 45$ and $x - 11 > -21$

20) $-7 < x - 9 < 8$

bit.ly/3RAbyde

Solutions at

✍ **Write the slope-intercept from equation of the following graph.**

21)

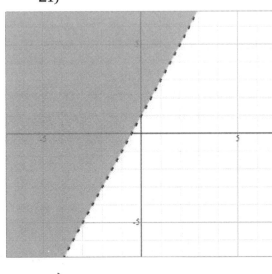

23)

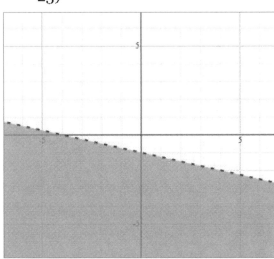

22)

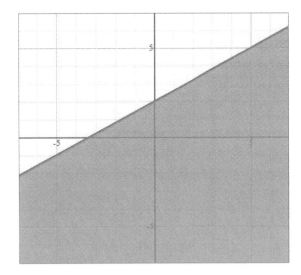

24)

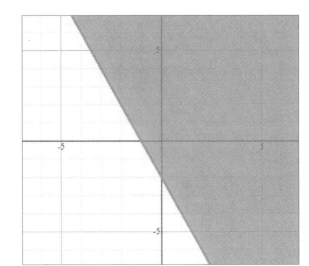

✍ **Solve the following inequality and graph the solution.**

25) $10 + 6p \leq -2$

26) $-r + 8 \leq 4$

27) $-2f + 10 \geq 6$

28) $1 + 3p > 7$

✍ **Solve each inequality.**

29) $8x - 3 \geq 4y + 2$

30) $4x - 3 \geq 5y + x$

31) $y \leq \frac{3}{2}x + 4$

32) $5x - 2y \leq 10$

✍ **Graph the solution of each inequality.**

33) $7x + 3 \geq 1 - 2x$

34) $\frac{x+4}{-4} > 8x + 2$

✍ **Solve each inequality.**

35) $|x| - 4 < 17$

36) $6 + |x - 8| > 15$

37) $\left|\frac{x}{2} + 3\right| > 6$

38) $\left|\frac{x+5}{4}\right| < 7$

✍ **Solve each system of equations.**

39) $\begin{cases} -2x + 2y = -4 & x = \\ 4x - 9y = 28 & y = \end{cases}$

40) $\begin{cases} x + 8y = -5 & x = \\ 2x + 6y = 0 & y = \end{cases}$

41) $\begin{cases} 4x - 3y = -2 & x = \\ x - y = 3 & y = \end{cases}$

42) $\begin{cases} 2x + 9y = 17 & x = \\ -3x + 8y = 39 & y = \end{cases}$

✍ **How many solutions does the following equation have?**

43) $4n = 8 + 5n$

44) $5 - 9f = -9f$

45) $0 = 3z - 3z$

46) $-9x + 2 = -9x$

47) $20 + 12y = 11y$

48) $10h - 2 = -4h$

✎ **Write a system of equations for the following graph.**

49)

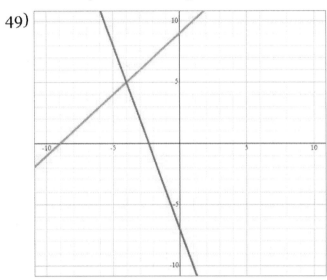

50)

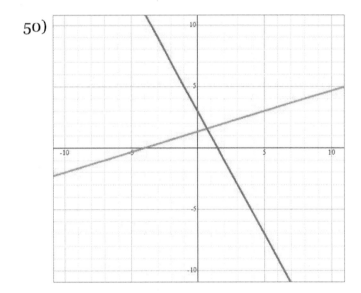

✎ **Solve each word problem.**

51) The equations of two lines are $3x - y = 7$ and $2x + 3y = 1$. What is the value of x in the solution for this system of equations?

52) The perimeter of a rectangle is 100 feet. The rectangle's length is 10 feet less than 5 times its width. What are the length and width of the rectangle?

🖎 Solve each word problem.

53) A golf club charges \$150 to join the club and \$15 for every hour using the driving range. Write an equation to express the cost C in terms of h hours playing tennis.

54) Susan is twice as old as Jane. In 4 years, Susan will be 24 years old. How old is Jane now?

55) A movie ticket costs \$7. Popcorn costs \$3 more than the ticket. If Alex bought 1 movie ticket and 1 popcorn, how much did he spend in total?

🖎 Solve each system of inequalities and graph them.

56) $\begin{cases} x + 2y \leq 3 \\ y - x \geq 0 \\ y \geq -2 \end{cases}$

57) $\begin{cases} x < 3 \\ x + y > -2 \\ y - 1 \leq x \end{cases}$

🖎 Solve each word problem.

58) James used his first 2 tokens in Glimmer Arcade to play a Roll-and-Score game. Then he played his favorite game, Balloon Bouncer, over and over until he ran out of tickets. Balloon Bouncer costs 4 tokens per game and James started the game with a bucket of 38 tokens. Write an equation James can use to find how many games of Balloon Bouncer, g, he played.

59) Sara buys juice and soda for the party and wants to spend no more than \$46. The price of each bottle of soda is 3 dollars and each bottle of fruit juice is 1 dollar. Write the inequality in a standard form that describes this situation. Use the given numbers and variables below.

x = the number of bottles of soda

y = the number of bottles of juice

Chapter 9: Answers

1) $x \geq 0$

2) $x < 6$

3) $x > -9$

4) $x > -1$

5) $x \leq 19$

6) $x \leq 2$

7) $x \leq 3$

8) $x \geq -6$

9) $x \geq -12$

10) $x < 3$

11) $x < -5$

12) $x \geq -9$

13) $x \geq -2$

14) $x < -6$

15) $x \geq -8$

16) $x > -6$

17) $x > -16$

18) $x < 2$

19) $-10 < x \leq 9$

20) $2 < x < 17$

21) $y > 2x + 1$

22) $y \leq \frac{3}{5}x + 2$

23) $y < -\frac{1}{4}x - 1$

24) $y \geq -2x - 2$

25) $p \leq -2$

26) $r \geq 4$

27) $f \leq 2$

28) $p > 2$

29) $\{(x, y) | y \in R, x \geq \frac{4y+5}{8}\}$

30) $\{(x, y) | y \in R, x \geq \frac{5y+3}{3}\}$

31) $\{(x, y) | y \in R, x \geq \frac{2y-8}{3}\}$

32) $\{(x, y) | y \in R, x \leq \frac{2y+10}{5}\}$

33) $x \geq -\frac{2}{9}$

34) $x < -\frac{4}{11}$

35) $-21 < x < 21$

36) $x > 17$ or $x < -1$

37) $x > 6$ or $x < -18$

38) $-33 < x < 23$

39) $x = -2, y = -4$

40) $x = 3, y = -1$

41) $x = -11, y = -14$

42) $x = -5, y = 3$

43) One solution

44) No solution

45) Infinitely solutions

46) No solution

47) One solution

48) One solution

49) $\begin{cases} y = -3x - 7 \\ y = x + 9 \end{cases}$

50) $\begin{cases} 2x + y = 3 \\ -x + 3y = 4 \end{cases}$

51) $x = 2$

52) $10, 40$

53) $C = 15h + 150$

54) 10

55) $\$17$

56) $\begin{cases} y \le -\frac{1}{2}x + \frac{3}{2} \\ y \ge x \\ y \ge -2 \end{cases}$

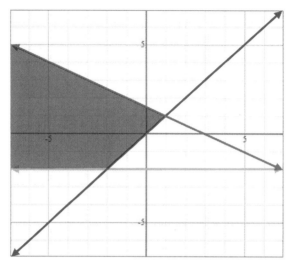

57) $\begin{cases} x < 3 \\ y > -x - 2 \\ y \le x + 1 \end{cases}$

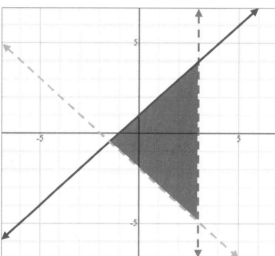

58) $4g + 2 = 38$

59) $3x + y \le 46$

10 Quadratic

Math topics that you'll learn in this chapter:

- ☑ Solving a Quadratic Equations
- ☑ Graphing Quadratic Functions
- ☑ Solve a Quadratic Equation by Factoring
- ☑ Transformations of Quadratic Functions
- ☑ Quadratic Formula and the Discriminant
- ☑ Characteristics of Quadratic Functions: Equations
- ☑ Characteristics of Quadratic Functions: Graphs
- ☑ Complete a Function Table: Quadratic Functions
- ☑ Domain and Range of Quadratic Functions: Equations
- ☑ Factor Quadratics: Special Cases
- ☑ Factor Quadratics Using Algebra Tiles
- ☑ Write a Quadratic Function from Its Vertex and Another Point

123

Solving a Quadratic Equations

- Write the equation in the form of: $ax^2 + bx + c = 0$.

- Factorize the quadratic, set each factor equal to zero and solve.

- Use quadratic formula if you can't factorize the quadratic.

- Quadratic formula: $x_{1,2} = \frac{-b \pm \sqrt{b^2 - 4ac}}{2a}$.

Examples:

Find the solutions of each quadratic.

Example 1. $x^2 + 7x + 12 = 0$.

Solution: Factor the quadratic by grouping. We need to find two numbers whose sum is 7 (from $7x$) and whose product is 12. Those numbers are 3 and 4. Then:

$$x^2 + 7x + 12 = 0 \rightarrow x^2 + 3x + 4x + 12 = 0 \rightarrow (x^2 + 3x) + (4x + 12) = 0.$$

Now, find common factors: $(x^2 + 3x) = x(x + 3)$ and $(4x + 12) = 4(x + 3)$. We have two expressions $(x^2 + 3x)$ and $(4x + 12)$ and their common factor is $(x + 3)$. Then: $(x^2 + 3x) + (4x + 12) = 0 \rightarrow x(x + 3) + 4(x + 3) = 0 \rightarrow (x + 3)(x + 4) = 0$.

The product of two expressions is 0. Then:

$$(x + 3) = 0 \rightarrow x = -3 \text{ or } (x + 4) = 0 \rightarrow x = -4.$$

Example 2. $x^2 + 5x + 6 = 0$.

Solution: Use quadratic formula: $x_{1,2} = \frac{-b \pm \sqrt{b^2 - 4ac}}{2a}$, $a = 1$, $b = 5$ and $c = 6$.

Then: $x_{1,2} = \frac{-5 \pm \sqrt{5^2 - 4 \times 1(6)}}{2(1)}$,

$$x_1 = \frac{-5 + \sqrt{5^2 - 4 \times 1(6)}}{2(1)} = -2, \ x_2 = \frac{-5 - \sqrt{5^2 - 4 \times 1(6)}}{2(1)} = -3.$$

Example 3. $x^2 + 6x + 8 = 0$.

Solution: Factor: $x^2 + 6x + 8 = 0 \rightarrow (x + 2)(x + 4) = 0 \rightarrow x = -2$, or $x = -4$.

Graphing Quadratic Functions

- Quadratic functions in vertex form: $y = a(x-h)^2 + k$ where (h, k) is the vertex of the function. The axis of symmetry is $x = h$.

- Quadratic functions in standard form: $y = ax^2 + bx + c$ where $x = -\frac{b}{2a}$ is the value of x in the vertex of the function.

- To graph a quadratic function, first find the vertex, then substitute some values for x and solve for y. (Remember that the graph of a quadratic function is a U−shaped curve and it is called "parabola".)

Example:

Sketch the graph of $y = (x + 2)^2 - 3$.

Solution:

Quadratic functions in vertex form:

$$y = a(x-h)^2 + k,$$

and (h, k) is the vertex.

Then, the vertex of $y = (x + 2)^2 - 3$ is:

$$(-2, -3).$$

Substitute zero for x and solve for y:

$$y = (0 + 2)^2 - 3 = 1.$$

The y − intercept is $(0,1)$.

Now, you can simply graph the quadratic function. Notice that quadratic function is a U−shaped curve.

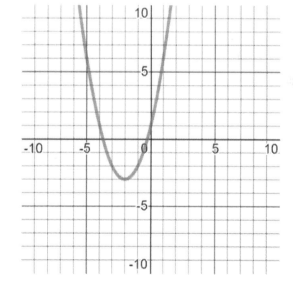

Solve a Quadratic Equation by Factoring

- The general form of a quadratic equation is: $ax^2 + bx + c = 0$.

- When factoring a quadratic equation, we can usually use the multiplication property of zero (MPZ).

    MPZ states that if $p \times q = 0$, then either $p = 0$ or $q = 0$.

- When there are only two terms and they have a common factor, then factoring is relatively simple. This is true of quadratic equations in the form $ax^2 + bx = 0$. (In this equation, the value of c is 0.) The two terms have at least a common factor of x. In this case, first find the greatest common factor (GCF) and factor it out. Then, use the multiplication property of zero (MPZ) to solve the equation.

Examples:

Example 1. Find the solutions of $x^2 - 7x = 0$.

Solution: The greatest common factor of the two terms is x.

Take the common factor out:

$$x(x - 7) = 0.$$

Using MPZ, which states that either $x = 0$ or $x - 7 = 0$.

In the second equation, the value of x equals 7.

$$x - 7 = 0 \rightarrow x = 7.$$

Example 2. Solve $x^2 + 10x - 24 = 0$ by factoring.

Solution: We first factorize the expression:

$$x^2 + 10x - 24 = (x + 12)(x - 2) = 0.$$

Using MPZ, which states that either $(x + 12) = 0$ or $(x - 2) = 0$.

$$(x + 12) = 0 \rightarrow x = -12, (x - 2) = 0 \rightarrow x = 2.$$

Transformations of Quadratic Functions

- In the quadratic equation $y = ax^2$, the graph stretches vertically by the value of unit a. Note that if a is negative, the graph will be inverted.

- In the vertex form, the quadratic function is as follows:

$$f(x) = a(x - h)^2 + k.$$

- In this case, point (h, k) is the vertex of the graph.

- If $k > 0$, the graph moves upwards, and if $k < 0$, the graph moves down.

- If $h > 0$, the graph moves to the right, and if $h < 0$, the graph moves to the left.

- The value of a indicates the elongation of the graph.

   ❖ If $|a| > 1$, the point corresponding to a certain value x moves farther from the $x-$axis, so the graph becomes thinner and there will be a vertical elongation.
   ❖ If $|a| < 1$, the point corresponding to a certain value of x gets closer to the $x-$axis, so the graph will be wider.

Example:

State the transformations and sketch the graph of the following function.

$$y = -3(x + 2)^2 + 4$$

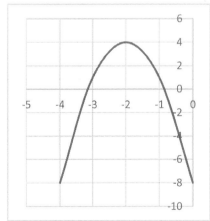

Solution: In this example, since $x - h = x + 2$, then $h = -2$. In this equation, $a = -3$, $h = -2$ and $k = 4$. Since $a < 0$, there is a downward parabola. The vertex is at $(-2, 4)$. Find the vertex and some other points to graph the parabola. The negative sign indicates a reflection over the $x-$axis. The parabola is vertically stretched by a factor of 3.

The parabola is shifted 2 units to the left. The parabola is shifted 4 units upward.

$x = 0 \rightarrow y = -3(0 + 2)^2 + 4 = -8,$

$x = -1 \rightarrow y = -3(-1 + 2)^2 + 4 = 1,$

$x = -3 \rightarrow y = -3(-3 + 2)^2 + 4 = 1.$

Quadratic Formula and the Discriminant

- A quadratic equation is in the form of $ax^2 + bx + c = 0$. To solve a quadratic equation by the delta (discriminant) method, go through the following steps:

Step 1: Calculate the delta number as follows: $\Delta = b^2 - 4ac$.

Step 2: Depending on the value of delta, there are three possible outcomes:

- If $\Delta < 0$, then the quadratic equation has no real roots.
- If $\Delta > 0$, then the quadratic equation has two roots, which are obtained by the following formulas:
$$x_1 = \frac{-b - \sqrt{\Delta}}{2a} \text{ and } x_2 = \frac{-b + \sqrt{\Delta}}{2a}.$$
- If $\Delta = 0$, then the two roots of the equation are equal and are called double roots:
$$x_1 = x_2 = \frac{-b}{2a}$$

Examples:

Example 1. Solve equation $5x^2 + 6x + 1 = 0$.

Solution: To solve a quadratic equation, first find the values of a, b, c.
By comparing the mentioned equation with the equation $ax^2 + bx + c = 0$, the values a, b, c are equal to: $a = 5$, $b = 6$, $c = 1$.
Now, calculate delta (Δ). Given the values of a, b, c, the value of Δ is equal to:
$$\Delta = b^2 - 4ac = 6^2 - 4 \times 5 \times 1 = 16.$$
16 is a positive number. Therefore, this equation will have two different solutions:
$$x = \frac{-6 \pm \sqrt{16}}{10} \rightarrow x = \frac{-6 \pm 4}{10} \rightarrow x = -\frac{1}{5}, \text{ or } x = -1.$$

Example 2. Find the solutions of the equation $5x^2 + 2x + 1 = 0$.

Solution: In the equation, the values of a, b, c are: $a = 5$, $b = 2$, $c = 1$.
$$\Delta = b^2 - 4ac = 2^2 - 4 \times 5 \times 1 = -16.$$
The value of delta is negative; Therefore, this equation has no solution in real numbers.

Characteristics of Quadratic Functions: Equations

- Using the equation of a quadratic function, the following can be determined.

  • Direction
  • Vertex
  • Axis of symmetry
  • x −intercept(s)
  • y −intercept
  • range
  • minimum/maximum value

Example:

Specify characteristics of the vertex, direction, and y −intercept for the quadratic function $f(x) = 2x^2 - 3x + 1$.

Solution: In the standard form of a quadratic function $f(x) = ax^2 + bx + c$, the vertex is not immediately obvious. The x −coordinate for the vertex can be obtained by using the formula: $x = -\dfrac{b}{2a}$,

$$x = -\frac{-3}{2(2)} = \frac{3}{4}$$

Now, substitute it into the equation of function to obtain the y −coordinate:

$$y = f\left(\frac{3}{4}\right) = 2\left(\frac{3}{4}\right)^2 - 3\left(\frac{3}{4}\right) + 1$$

$$= 2\left(\frac{9}{16}\right) - \frac{9}{4} + 1$$

$$= \frac{9}{8} - \frac{9}{4} + 1 = -\frac{1}{8}.$$

So, the vertex of the function $f(x) = 2x^2 - 3x + 1$ is the ordered pair $\left(\frac{3}{4}, -\frac{1}{8}\right)$.

Remember that the sign of the coefficient x^2 indicates the direction of the quadratic equation. Since the coefficient of x^2 is 2, then it is upward.

To find the y −intercept of a function, evaluate the output at $f(0)$.

$$f(0) = 2(0)^2 - 3(0) + 1 = 1.$$

Characteristics of Quadratic Functions: Graphs

- From the graph of a quadratic function, determine the:

  - vertex

  - axis of symmetry

  - x −intercepts

  - y −intercept

  - domain

  - range

  - minimum/maximum value

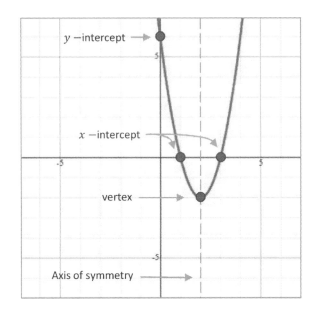

Example:

Considering the following graph,

determine the following:

- vertex

- axis of symmetry

- x −intercepts

- y −intercept

- Max/minimum point.

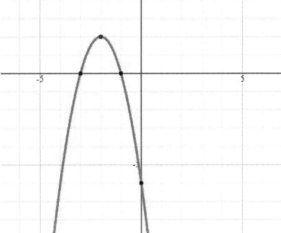

Solution: According to the graph, see that

a point at the coordinate $(-2,2)$ is the vertex. So, the line $x = -2$ is the axis of symmetry.

Since the graph intersects the x −axis at points -1 and -3, the mentioned points are

x −intercepts. In the same way, the point $(0, -6)$ is the y −intercept.

In addition, this is clear that the vertex is the maximum point.

Complete a Function Table: Quadratic Functions

- To complete a function table of the quadratic function:

   Step 1: Consider the input and output in the table.

   Step 2: Substitute the input into the function.

   Step 3: Evaluate the output.

Example:

Complete the table.

$g(t) = t^2 - 2t + 1$	
t	$g(t)$
-1	
0	
1	

Solution: According to the function table, the first value of the input in the table is -1. Evaluate $g(t) = t^2 - 2t + 1$ for $t = -1$.

$$g(-1) = (-1)^2 - 2(-1) + 1$$

$$= 1 + 2 + 1 = 4.$$

$g(t) = t^2 - 2t + 1$	
t	$g(t)$
-1	4
0	
1	

When $t = -1$, then $g(-1) = 4$. Complete the first row of the table.

In the same way, evaluate $g(t) = t^2 - 2t + 1$ for $t = 0$ and $t = 1$, respectively. So,

$$g(0) = (0)^2 - 2(0) + 1 = 1,$$

$$g(1) = (1)^2 - 2(1) + 1 = 0.$$

$g(t) = t^2 - 2t + 1$	
t	$g(t)$
-1	4
0	1
1	0

Enter the obtained values in the table.

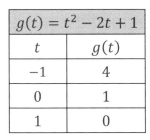

Find more at

bit.ly/3XlOVuF

Domain and Range of Quadratic Functions

- The domain of any quadratic function in the form $y = ax^2 + bx + c$ (where a, b, and c are constants) is the set of all real numbers.

- To find the range of a quadratic function, you need to first identify the vertex of the parabola and determine whether it opens upwards or downwards. If the coefficient a is positive ($a > 0$), the parabola opens upwards, and the vertex is the minimum point of the function. Conversely, if a is negative or ($a < 0$) the parabola opens downwards, and the vertex is the maximum point of the function.

- The vertex of a quadratic function can be found using the formula:
Vertex $(h, k) = (-\frac{b}{2a}, f(-\frac{b}{2a}))$.

Example:

What is the domain and range of the function to the equation?

$$y = x^2 - 2x + 1.$$

Solution: To find the domain and range of the function $y = x^2 - 2x + 1$, we'll first identify the vertex and determine the direction of the parabola.

The vertex of a quadratic function can be found using the formula:

$$\text{Vertex } (h, k) = (-\frac{b}{2a}, f(-\frac{b}{2a})).$$

In our case, the quadratic function is $y = x^2 - 2x + 1$, where $a = 1$, $b = -2$, and $c = 1$.

$$h = -\frac{(-2)}{2 \times 1} = \frac{2}{2} = 1, k = f(h) = f(1) = (1)^2 - 2(1) + 1 = 1 - 2 + 1 = 0$$

So, the vertex of the parabola is $(1, 0)$.

No, we need to identify the direction of the parabola. Since the coefficient a is positive ($a = 1 > 0$), the parabola opens upwards, and the vertex is the minimum point of the function.

The domain of a quadratic function is all real numbers since it is defined for every x value. Therefore, the domain is: Domain $= \{x \mid x \in R\}$

The range is determined by the direction of the parabola and the vertex. Since the parabola opens upwards, the range will include all values greater than or equal to the y −coordinate (k) of the vertex. In this case, the range will be: Range $= \{y \mid y \geq 0\}$

Factor Quadratics: Special Cases

- Special cases square:

  • Factor an equation of the form: $a^2 \pm 2ab + b^2 = (a \pm b)^2$

  • Factor an equation of the form: $a^2 - b^2 = (a + b)(a - b)$

Examples:

Example 1. Factor $4x^2 - 36$.

Solution: Notice that $4x^2$ and 36 are perfect squares, because $4x^2 = (2x)^2$, and $36 = 6^2$. By using the formula $a^2 - b^2 = (a + b)(a - b)$. Let $a = 2x$, and $b = 6$. The represented equation can be rewritten as follows:

$$4x^2 - 36 = (2x + 6)(2x - 6).$$

Example 2. Factor $4k^2 - 4k + 1$.

Solution: First, consider that this formula $a^2 - 2ab + b^2 = (a - b)^2$. Since $4k^2 = (2k)^2$, then $4k^2$ and 1 are perfect squares. This means that $a = 2k$, and $b = 1$. Next, check to see if the middle term is equal to $2ab$, which it is: $2ab = 2(2k)1 = 4k$. Therefore, the square equation can be rewritten as,

$$4k^2 - 4k + 1 = (2k - 1)^2.$$

Example 3. Factor $36x^2 + 36x + 9$.

Solution: First, notice that $36x^2$ and 9 are perfect squares because $36x^2 = (6x)^2$ and $9 = 3^2$. Let $a = 6x$, and $b = 3$. Now, evaluate the middle term $36x$. Then, you can write as $36x = 2(6x)3 = 2ab$. Using this formula: $a^2 + 2ab + b^2 = (a + b)^2$.

Therefore, we have:

$$36x^2 + 36x + 9 = (6x + 3)^2.$$

Example 4. Factor $2x^2 - 16x + 32$.

Solution: First, rewrite the equation as $2x^2 - 16x + 32 = 2(x^2 - 8x + 16)$. According to the x^2 and 16 are perfect squares because $x^2 = (x)^2$ and $16 = 4^2$. That is, $a = x$, and $b = 4$. Now, check to see if the middle term is equal to $2ab$: $2ab = 2(x)4 = 8x$. Using this formula: $a^2 + 2ab + b^2 = (a + b)^2$.

Therefore, we have: $2x^2 - 16x + 32 = 2(x^2 - 8x + 16) = 2(x - 4)^2$.

bit.ly/3VTKoxQ

Find more at

Factor Quadratics Using Algebra Tiles

- To factor quadratic expressions like $ax^2 + bx + c$ using algebraic tiles, follow the steps below:

- Model the polynomials with tiles.

- Arrange the tiles into a rectangle grid. Start with the x^2 tiles from the upper left corner so that the number of horizontal and vertical divisions is equal to the multiples of a. Add the integer tiles in the lower right corner. Here, the number of horizontal and vertical divisions should be equal to integer multiples. Make sure to choose horizontal and vertical divisions from possible multiples of a and c that will fill the remaining empty grid tiles.

- The product of expressions related to horizontal and vertical divisions is equal to the answer.

- Check the answer.

Example:

Use algebra tiles to factor: $3x^2 - 7x + 2$.

Solution: Model the polynomials with tiles:

In this case, arrange the tiles into a rectangle grid.

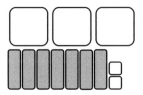

Determine both binomials relate to the divisions, such that $3x - 1$ for the horizontal division and $x - 2$ for the vertical. As follow:

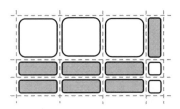

In the end, multiply two expressions and check the answer,

$$(3x - 1)(x - 2) = 3x^2 - 7x + 2.$$

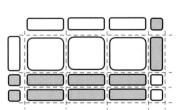

Write a Quadratic Function from Its Vertex and Another Point

- A quadratic function in the standard form of $y = ax^2 + bx + c$ can be represented in the vertex form as follows:

$$y = a(x - h)^2 + k,$$

where (h, k) is the coordinate of the vertex.

- So that if $a > 0$, the function opens up and the coordinate vertex is the minimum value of the function. If $a < 0$, then the function is downward, and the coordinate vertex is the maximum value.

Examples:

Example 1. A quadratic function opening up or down has vertex $(0,1)$ and passes through $(2,0)$. Write its equation in vertex form.

Solution: Use the vertex form of the quadratic function as $y = a(x - h)^2 + k$. Put the coordinate of the vertex $(0,1)$ in the vertex form:

$$(0,1) \rightarrow 1 = a(x - 0)^2 + 1 \rightarrow y = ax^2 + 1.$$

To find a, substitute $(2,0)$ in this equation and calculate. Then,

$$(2,0) \rightarrow 0 = a(2)^2 + 1 \rightarrow a = -\frac{1}{4}.$$

Therefore, the equation of the quadratic function in the vertex form is as follows:

$$y = -\frac{1}{4}x^2 + 1.$$

Example 2. A quadratic function has vertex $(0,0)$ and passes through $(-12, -18)$. Write its equation in vertex form.

Solution: By using the vertex form formula: $y = a(x - h)^2 + k$. So, we have:

$$(0,0) \rightarrow y = a(x - 0)^2 + 0 \rightarrow y = ax^2.$$

Substitute $(-12, -18)$ in the obtained equation, then:

$$-18 = a(-12)^2 \rightarrow -18 = 144a \rightarrow a = -\frac{18}{144} = -\frac{1}{8}.$$

Therefore, $y = -\frac{1}{8}x^2$.

bit.ly/3XLDlc7

Find more at

Chapter 10: Practices

✎ **Solve each equation by factoring or using the quadratic formula**.

1) $x^2 - x - 2 = 0$

2) $x^2 - 6x + 8 = 0$

3) $x^2 - 4x + 3 = 0$

4) $x^2 + x - 12 = 0$

5) $x^2 + 7x - 18 = 0$

6) $x^2 - 2x - 15 = 0$

7) $x^2 + 6x - 40 = 0$

8) $x^2 - 9x - 36 = 0$

✎ **Sketch the graph of each function.**

9) $y = (x - 4)^2 - 2$

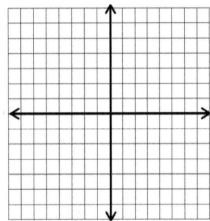

10) $y = 2(x + 2)^2 - 3$

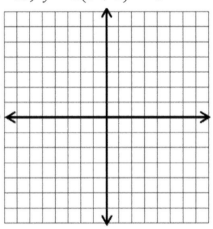

✎ **Solve each equation by factoring or using the quadratic formula.**

11) $x^2 - 2x - 3 = 0$

12) $x^2 + 9x + 20 = 0$

✎ **State the transformations and sketch the graph of the following function.**

13) $y = 2(x - 3)^2 + 1$

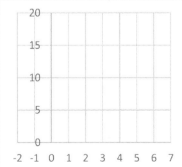

Find the answer to the equation.

14) $2x^2 - 7x + 3 = 0$

15) $x^2 + 8x - 9 = 0$

16) $2x^2 + 5x - 3 = 0$

17) $x^2 + 6x + 9 = 0$

Solve.

18) Find the equation of the axis of symmetry for the parabola $y = x^2 + 7x + 3$.

19) Find the y-intercept of the parabola $x^2 + 25x + 7$.

20) Find the vertex of the parabola $y = x^2 - 4x + 3$.

Considering the following graph, determine the following:

21) vertex

22) axis of symmetry

23) $y -$intercepts

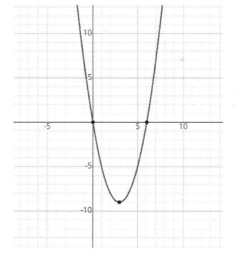

Complete the table.

24)

$g(t) = t^2 + 7$	
t	$g(t)$
-1	
0	
1	

25)

$f(p) = 4p^2$	
p	$f(p)$
-2	
0	
2	

✍ **Determine the domain and range of each function.**

26) $y = x^2 + 5x + 6$

27) $y = x^2 + 3$

28) $y = -x^2 + 4$

✍ **Factor.**

29) $25x^2 + 20x + 4$ 31) $3 + 6x + 3x^2$

30) $9x^2 - 1$ 32) $b^4 - 36$

✍ **Use algebra tiles to factor.**

33) $x^2 - 3x + 2$ 34) $x^2 + 5x + 6$

✍ **Write each quadratic function as a vertex form.**

35) A parabola opening or down has vertex $(0,0)$ and passes through $(8, -16)$.

36) A parabola opening up or down has vertex $(0, 2)$ and passes through $(-2,5)$.

Chapter 10: Answers

1) $x = 2, x = -1$

2) $x = 2, x = 4$

3) $x = 3, x = 1$

4) $x = 3, x = -4$

5) $x = 2, x = -9$

6) $x = 5, x = -3$

7) $x = 4, x = -10$

8) $x = 12, x = -3$

9) $y = (x - 4)^2 - 2$

10) $y = 2(x + 2)^2 - 3$

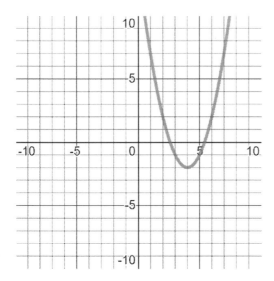
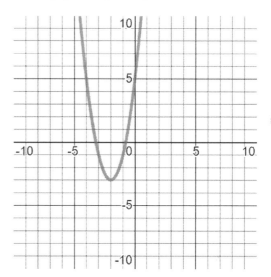

11) $\{3, -1\}$

12) $\{-4, -5\}$

13) The graph stretches vertically by a factor of 2.

Move 3 units to the right and 1 unit up.

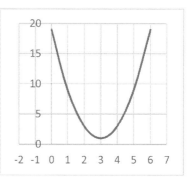

14) $x_1 = 3, x_2 = \frac{1}{2}$

15) $x_1 = -9, x_2 = 1$

16) $x_1 = -3, x_2 = \frac{1}{2}$

17) $x_1 = x_2 = -3$

18) $x = -\frac{7}{2}$

19) 7

20) $(2, -1)$

21) $(3, -9)$

22) 3

23) 0

24)

$g(t) = t^2 + 7$	
t	$g(t)$
-1	8
0	7
1	8

25)

$f(p) = 4p^2$	
p	$f(p)$
-2	16
0	0
2	16

26) $D = \{x|x \in R\}, R = \{y \in R|y \geq -0.25\}$

27) $D = \{x|x \in R\}, R = \{R|y \geq 3\}$

28) $D = \{x|x \in R\}, R = \{y \in R|y \leq 4\}$

29) $(5x + 2)^2$

30) $(3x - 1)(3x + 1)$

31) $3(1 + x)^2$

32) $(b^2 + 6)(b^2 - 6)$

33) $(x - 1)(x - 2)$

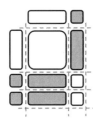

34) $(x + 2)(x + 3)$

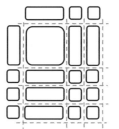

35) $y = -\frac{1}{4}x^2$

36) $y = \frac{3}{4}x^2 + 2$

CHAPTER

11 Polynomials

Math topics that you'll learn in this chapter:

- ☑ Simplifying Polynomials
- ☑ Adding and Subtracting Polynomials
- ☑ Add and Subtract Polynomials Using Algebra Tiles
- ☑ Multiplying Monomials
- ☑ Multiplying and Dividing Monomials
- ☑ Multiplying a Polynomial and a Monomial
- ☑ Multiply Polynomials Using Area Models
- ☑ Multiplying Binomials
- ☑ Multiply two Binomials Using Algebra Tiles
- ☑ Factoring Trinomials
- ☑ Factoring Polynomials
- ☑ Use a Graph to Factor Polynomials
- ☑ Factoring Special Case Polynomials
- ☑ Add Polynomials to Find Perimeter

123

Simplifying Polynomials

- To simplify polynomials, find "like" terms. (They have the same variables with the same power).

- Use "FOIL". (First–Out–In–Last) for binomials:

$$(x + a)(x + b) = x^2 + (b + a)x + ab$$

- Add or subtract "like" terms using order of operation.

Examples:

Example 1. Simplify this expression. $x(4x + 7) - 2x =$

Solution: Use the Distributive Property:

$$x(4x + 7) = 4x^2 + 7x.$$

Now, combine like terms:

$$x(4x + 7) - 2x = 4x^2 + 7x - 2x = 4x^2 + 5x.$$

Example 2. Simplify this expression. $(x + 3)(x + 5) =$

Solution: First, apply the FOIL method:

$$(a + b)(c + d) = ac + ad + bc + bd.$$

Therefore:

$$(x + 3)(x + 5) = x^2 + 5x + 3x + 15.$$

Now combine like terms:

$$x^2 + 5x + 3x + 15 = x^2 + 8x + 15.$$

Example 3. Simplify this expression. $2x(x - 5) - 3x^2 + 6x =$.

Solution: Use the Distributive Property:

$$2x(x - 5) = 2x^2 - 10x.$$

Then:

$$2x(x - 5) - 3x^2 + 6x = 2x^2 - 10x - 3x^2 + 6x.$$

Now combine like terms:

$$2x^2 - 3x^2 = -x^2, \text{ and } -10x + 6x = -4x.$$

The simplified form of the expression:

$$2x^2 - 10x - 3x^2 + 6x = -x^2 - 4x.$$

Adding and Subtracting Polynomials

- Adding polynomials is just a matter of combining like terms, with some order of operations considerations thrown in.

- Be careful with the minus signs, and don't confuse addition and multiplication!

- For subtracting polynomials, sometimes you need to use the Distributive Property: $a(b + c) = ab + ac$, $a(b - c) = ab - ac$.

Examples:

Example 1. Simplify the expressions. $(x^2 - 2x^3) - (x^3 - 3x^2) =$

Solution: First, use the Distributive Property: $-(x^3 - 3x^2) = -x^3 + 3x^2$.
$\rightarrow (x^2 - 2x^3) - (x^3 - 3x^2) = x^2 - 2x^3 - x^3 + 3x^2$.
Now combine like terms: $-2x^3 - x^3 = -3x^3$ and $x^2 + 3x^2 = 4x^2$.
Then: $(x^2 - 2x^3) - (x^3 - 3x^2) = x^2 - 2x^3 - x^3 + 3x^2 = -3x^3 + 4x^2$

Example 2. Add expressions. $(3x^3 - 5) + (4x^3 - 2x^2) =$

Solution: Remove parentheses:
$(3x^3 - 5) + (4x^3 - 2x^2) = 3x^3 - 5 + 4x^3 - 2x^2$.
Now combine like terms: $3x^3 - 5 + 4x^3 - 2x^2 = 7x^3 - 2x^2 - 5$.

Example 3. Simplify the expressions. $(-4x^2 - 2x^3) - (5x^2 + 2x^3) =$

Solution: First, use the Distributive Property: $-(5x^2 + 2x^3) = -5x^2 - 2x^3 \rightarrow$
$(-4x^2 - 2x^3) - (5x^2 + 2x^3) = -4x^2 - 2x^3 - 5x^2 - 2x^3$.
Now combine like terms and write in standard form:
$-4x^2 - 2x^3 - 5x^2 - 2x^3 = -4x^3 - 9x^2$.

Example 4. Simplify the expressions. $(8x^2 - 3x^3) + (2x^2 + 5x^3) =$

Solution: Remove parentheses:

$(8x^2 - 3x^3) + (2x^2 + 5x^3) = 8x^2 - 3x^3 + 2x^2 + 5x^3$.

Now combine like terms and write in standard form:

$8x^2 - 3x^3 + 2x^2 + 5x^3 = 10x^2 + 2x^3 = 2x^3 + 10x^2$.

bit.ly/2KUqHqQ
Find more at

Add and Subtract Polynomials Using Algebra Tiles

- To better understand and visualize the addition and subtraction of algebraic expressions, you can use Algebra tiles as follow:

- Model the polynomials using tiles.
- For algebraic subtraction, change the color of the tiles on the second side.
- Cross out the same number of negative or positive tiles on both sides of the equation.
- Write the answer by determining the number of remaining tiles.

Examples

Example 1. Use algebra tiles to simplify: $(x^2 - x + 3) + (2x^2 + 3x - 2)$.

Solution: Model the given polynomials using algebra tiles.

Here, cross out one x tile on the left side and do the same on the other side. In the same way, cancel two 1 tiles on the left side and do the same on the right side. That is,

Count the number of remaining tiles. So, $3x^2 + 2x + 1$.

Example 2. Simplify the polynomial $(2x^2 + 3x - 1) - (x^2 - 2x - 2)$ using algebra tiles.

Solution: Model the polynomials with tiles.

Change the color of the tiles on the second side, then add them to the first side.

Now, simplify the obtained algebraic tiles by canceling negative and positive tiles of the same size. As follow:

Finally, by counting the remaining tiles, the following expression obtains: $x^2 + 5x + 1$.

Multiplying Monomials

- A monomial is a polynomial with just one term: Examples: $2x$ or $7y^2$.

- When you multiply monomials, first multiply the coefficients (a number placed before) and then multiply the variables using multiplication property of exponents.

$$x^a \times x^b = x^{a+b}$$

Examples:

Example 1. Multiply expressions. $2xy^3 \times 6x^4y^2$.

Solution: Find the same variables and use the multiplication property of exponents: $x^a \times x^b = x^{a+b}$.

$x \times x^4 = x^{1+4} = x^5$ and $y^3 \times y^2 = y^{3+2} = y^5$.

Then, multiply coefficients and variables: $2xy^3 \times 6x^4y^2 = 12x^5y^5$.

Example 2. Multiply expressions. $7a^3b^8 \times 3a^6b^4 =$

Solution: Use the multiplication property of exponents: $x^a \times x^b = x^{a+b}$.

$a^3 \times a^6 = a^{3+6} = a^9$ and $b^8 \times b^4 = b^{8+4} = b^{12}$.

Then: $7a^3b^8 \times 3a^6b^4 = 21a^9b^{12}$.

Example 3. Multiply. $5x^2y^4z^3 \times 4x^4y^7z^5$

Solution: Use the multiplication property of exponents: $x^a \times x^b = x^{a+b}$.

$x^2 \times x^4 = x^{2+4} = x^6$, $y^4 \times y^7 = y^{4+7} = y^{11}$ and $z^3 \times z^5 = z^{3+5} = z^8$.

Then: $5x^2y^4z^3 \times 4x^4y^7z^5 = 20x^6y^{11}z^8$.

Example 4. Simplify. $(-6a^7b^4)(4a^8b^5) =$

Solution: Use the multiplication property of exponents: $x^a \times x^b = x^{a+b}$.

$a^7 \times a^8 = a^{7+8} = a^{15}$ and $b^4 \times b^5 = b^{4+5} = b^9$.

Then: $(-6a^7b^4)(4a^8b^5) = -24a^{15}b^9$.

bit.ly/2KLVoP8

Find more at

Multiplying and Dividing Monomials

- When you divide or multiply two monomials, you need to divide or multiply their coefficients and then divide or multiply their variables.

- In case of exponents with the same base, for Division, subtract their powers, for Multiplication, add their powers.

- Exponent's Multiplication and Division rules:

$$x^a \times x^b = x^{a+b}, \frac{x^a}{x^b} = x^{a-b}$$

Examples:

Example 1. Multiply expressions. $(3x^5)(9x^4) =$

Solution: Use the multiplication property of exponents:
$x^a \times x^b = x^{a+b} \rightarrow x^5 \times x^4 = x^9$, then: $(3x^5)(9x^4) = 27x^9$.

Example 2. Multiply expressions. $(-5x^8)(4x^6) =$

Solution: Use the multiplication property of exponents:

$x^a \times x^b = x^{a+b} \rightarrow x^8 \times x^6 = x^{14}$.

Then: $(-5x^8)(4x^6) = -20x^{14}$.

Example 3. Divide expressions. $\frac{12x^4y^6}{6xy^2} =$

Solution: Use the division property of exponents:
$\frac{x^a}{x^b} = x^{a-b} \rightarrow \frac{x^4}{x} = x^{4-1} = x^3$ and $\frac{y^6}{y^2} = y^{6-2} = y^4$.
Then: $\frac{12x^4y^6}{6xy^2} = 2x^3y^4$.

Example 4. Divide expressions. $\frac{49a^6b^9}{7a^3b^4}$

Solution: Use the division property of exponents:
$\frac{x^a}{x^b} = x^{a-b} \rightarrow \frac{a^6}{a^3} = a^{6-3} = a^3$ and $\frac{b^9}{b^4} = b^{9-4} = b^5$.
Then: $\frac{49a^6b^9}{7a^3b^4} = 7a^3b^5$.

Multiplying a Polynomial and a Monomial

- When multiplying monomials, use the product rule for exponents.

$$x^a \times x^b = x^{a+b}$$

- When multiplying a monomial by a polynomial, use the distributive property.

$$a \times (b + c) = a \times b + a \times c = ab + ac$$
$$a \times (b - c) = a \times b - a \times c = ab - ac$$

Examples:

Example 1. Multiply expressions. $6x(2x + 5)$

Solution: Use the Distributive Property:

$6x(2x + 5) = 6x \times 2x + 6x \times 5 = 12x^2 + 30x$.

Example 2. Multiply expressions. $x(3x^2 + 4y^2)$

Solution: Use the Distributive Property:

$x(3x^2 + 4y^2) = x \times 3x^2 + x \times 4y^2 = 3x^3 + 4xy^2$.

Example 3. Multiply. $-x(-2x^2 + 4x + 5)$

Solution: Use the Distributive Property:

$-x(-2x^2 + 4x + 5) = (-x) \times (-2x^2) + (-x) \times (4x) + (-x) \times (5) = 2x^3 - 4x^2 - 5x$.

Example 4. Multiply. $-4x(-5x^2 + 3x - 6)$

Solution: Use the Distributive Property:

$-4x(-5x^2 + 3x - 6) = (-4x) \times (-5x^2) + (-4x) \times (3x) + (-4x) \times (-6) = 20x^3 -$

$12x^2 + 24x$.

Multiply Polynomials Using Area Models

- To multiply polynomials using area models, follow the steps below:

  • Model a rectangular area such that each side corresponds to the polynomials.
  • Divide the sides associated with each of the polynomials. Separate each polynomial side into the monomial factors.
  • Complete the areas by multiplying the monomials.
  • To find the product of polynomials, add the resulting expressions.

Examples:

Example 1. Use the area model to find the product $2x(x + 1)$.

Solution: Model a rectangular area,

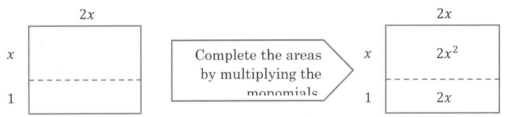

Last, combine terms to find the polynomial product.

$$2x(x + 1) = 2x^2 + 2x.$$

Example 2. Use an area model to multiply these binomials.

$$(a - 2)(3a + 1)$$

Solution: Draw an area model representing the product $(a - 2)(3a + 1)$.

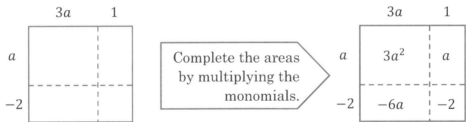

Now, add the partial products to find the product and simplify,

$$3a^2 + a - 6a - 2 = 3a^2 - 5a - 2.$$

Therefore, $(a - 2)(3a + 1) = 3a^2 - 5a - 2$.

bit.ly/3HnfiL0

Find more at

Multiplying Binomials

- A binomial is a polynomial that is the sum or the difference of two terms, each of which is a monomial.

- To multiply two binomials, use the "FOIL" method. (First–Out–In–Last)

$$(x + a)(x + b) = x \times x + x \times b + a \times x + a \times b = x^2 + bx + ax + ab$$

Examples:

Example 1. Multiply Binomials. $(x + 3)(x - 2) =$

Solution: Use the "FOIL". (First–Out–In–Last):

$(x + 3)(x - 2) = x^2 - 2x + 3x - 6.$

Then combine like terms: $x^2 - 2x + 3x - 6 = x^2 + x - 6.$

Example 2. Multiply. $(x + 6)(x + 4) =$

Solution: Use the "FOIL". (First–Out–In–Last):

$(x + 6)(x + 4) = x^2 + 4x + 6x + 24.$

Then simplify: $x^2 + 4x + 6x + 24 = x^2 + 10x + 24.$

Example 3. Multiply. $(x + 5)(x - 7) =$

Solution: Use the "FOIL". (First–Out–In–Last):

$(x + 5)(x - 7) = x^2 - 7x + 5x - 35.$

Then simplify: $x^2 - 7x + 5x - 35 = x^2 - 2x - 35.$

Example 4. Multiply Binomials. $(x - 9)(x - 5) =$

Solution: Use the "FOIL". (First–Out–In–Last):

$(x - 9)(x - 5) = x^2 - 5x - 9x + 45.$

Then combine like terms: $x^2 - 5x - 9x + 45 = x^2 - 14x + 45.$

bit.ly/3aCsOFL

Find more at

Multiply two Binomials Using Algebra Tiles

- To find the product of two binomials using algebraic tiles, do these in the following way:

    • Set up the grid so that the horizontal divisions correspond to one of the binomials and the vertical divisions to the other side.
    • Match the appropriate tiles in this grid.
    • To specify the answer, sum the like terms inside the grid.

- Remember these rules for performing the multiplication of binomials containing a negative term:

    • Two positives or two negatives equal a positive value.
    • A positive and a negative equal a negative value.

Example:

Use algebra tiles to simplify: $(x - 2)(2x + 1)$.

Solution: Set up the grid as follow:

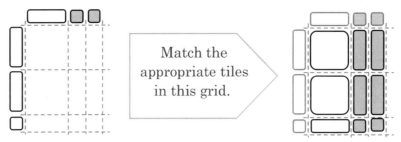

Here, cross out one x tile on the first column and do the same on the second column.

Count the like terms inside the grid. Since the number of x^2 tiles = 2, the number of

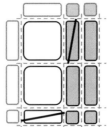

$-x$ tiles = 3, and the number of -1 tiles = 2, then, sum the like terms inside the grid.

So, $2x^2 - 3x - 2$.

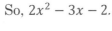

Factoring Trinomials

- To factor trinomials, you can use following methods:

  - "FOIL": $(x + a)(x + b) = x^2 + (b + a)x + ab$.

  - "Difference of Squares":

$$a^2 - b^2 = (a + b)(a - b)$$
$$a^2 + 2ab + b^2 = (a + b)(a + b)$$
$$a^2 - 2ab + b^2 = (a - b)(a - b)$$

  - "Reverse FOIL": $x^2 + (b + a)x + ab = (x + a)(x + b)$.

Examples:

Example 1. Factor this trinomial. $x^2 - 2x - 8$

Solution: Break the expression into groups. You need to find two numbers that their product is -8 and their sum is -2. (remember "Reverse FOIL": $x^2 + (b + a)x + ab = (x + a)(x + b)$). Those two numbers are 2 and -4. Then: $x^2 - 2x - 8 = (x^2 + 2x) + (-4x - 8)$.

Now factor out x from $x^2 + 2x$: $x(x + 2)$, and factor out -4 from $-4x - 8$: $-4(x + 2)$; then: $(x^2 + 2x) + (-4x - 8) = x(x + 2) - 4(x + 2)$

Now factor out like term: $(x + 2)$. Then: $(x + 2)(x - 4)$.

Example 2. Factor this trinomial. $x^2 - 2x - 24$

Solution: Break the expression into groups: $(x^2 + 4x) + (-6x - 24)$.

Now factor out x from $x^2 + 4x$: $x(x + 4)$, and factor out -6 from $-6x - 24$: $-6(x + 4)$; then: $x(x + 4) - 6(x + 4)$, now factor out like term: $(x + 4) \rightarrow x(x + 4) - 6(x + 4) = (x + 4)(x - 6)$.

bit.ly/38EpdJA

Find more at

Factoring Polynomials

- To factor a polynomial:

  • Step 1: Break down each term into its prime factors.

  • Step 2: Find GCF (greatest common factor).

  • Step 3: Factor the GCF out from each term.

  • Step 4: Simplify as needed.

  • To factor a polynomial, you can also use these formulas:

  $$(x + a)(x + b) = x^2 + (b + a)x + ab$$

  $$a^2 - b^2 = (a + b)(a - b)$$

  $$a^2 + 2ab + b^2 = (a + b)(a + b)$$

  $$a^2 - 2ab + b^2 = (a - b)(a - b)$$

Examples:

Factor each polynomial.

Example 1. $6x^3 - 6x$

Solution: To factorize the expression $6x^3 - 6x$, first factor out the largest common factor, $6x$, and then you will see that you have the pattern of the difference between two complete squares: $(a - b)(a + b) = a^2 - b^2$, then: $6x^3 - 6x = 6x(x^2 - 1) = 6x(x - 1)(x + 1)$.

Example 2. $x^2 + 9x + 20$

Solution: To factorize the expression $x^2 + 9x + 20$, you need to find two numbers whose product is 20 and sum is 9. You can get the number 20 by multiplying 1×20, 2×10, 4×5. The last pair will be your choice, because $4 + 5 = 9$.

Then: $x^2 + 9x + 20 = (x + 4)(x + 5)$.

bit.ly/3KH3xha

Find more at

Use a Graph to Factor Polynomials

- If a polynomial includes the factor of the form $(x - h)^p$, you can determine the behavior near the x −intercept by the power p. It can be said that $x = h$ is a zero of multiplicity p:
    • If a polynomial function graph touches the x −axis, it's zero with even multiplicity.
    • If a polynomial function' graph crosses the x −axis, it's a zero with odd multiplicity.
    • A polynomial function' graph gets flattered at zero if the multiplicity of the zero is higher.
    • The sum of the multiplicities of the zero is the polynomial function's degree.
- To check factorization using a graphing calculator, follow these steps:

    • 1ˢᵗ step: Press the $Y =$ button and enter the given equation for $Y1$.
    • 2ⁿᵈ step: Press the GRAPH button to see the equation's graph.
    • 3ʳᵈ step: Press the TRACE button and by the left and right buttons move the cursor along the graph. You can see at which points the graph crosses the x −axis
    • 4th step: To find the y −values at the x −values when the graph crosses the x −axis, enter the value of x at this point and press ENTER button while in Trace mode. The calculator finds the y −value for you. The calculator tells you that in these values of x the y −values are equal to zero.
    • 5th step: Remember that for functions with binomial factors of the form $(x - a)$, a is an x −intercept.

Example:

Use a graph to factor following polynomial.

$$x^2 - x - 2$$

Solution: First, graph the polynomial. Then find the points where the polynomial function graph crosses the x −axis. These points are the zeros of the polynomial function. For $x^2 - x - 2, x = -1$ and $x = 2$ are the zeros of the polynomial function.

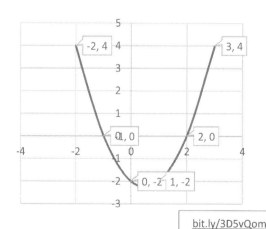

Factoring Special Case Polynomials

- There are different methods to factor a special polynomial. Here are some common polynomial cases to factor:

- To solve the difference between two complete squares:

$$x^2 - a^2 = (x - a)(x + a)$$

- To solve a perfect square trinomial:

$$a^2 + 2ab + b^2 = (a + b)^2$$

$$a^2 - 2ab + b^2 = (a - b)^2$$

- FOIL:

$$(x + a)(x + b) = x^2 + (b + a)x + ab$$

- Reverse FOIL:

$$x^2 + (b + a)x + ab = (x + a)(x + b)$$

Examples:

Example 1. Factor completely. $25y^2 + 30y + 9$

Solution: You may notice that two terms $25y^2$ and 9 are perfect squares. The root $25y^2$ is equal to $5y$, and the root 9 is equal to 3. The middle expression, $30y$, is equal to twice the product of $5y$ and 3. So, you have a perfect square trinomial whose factoring result is $(5y + 3)^2$.

$25y^2 + 30y + 9 = (5y + 3)^2$.

Example 2. Factor completely. $36y^2 - 25x^4$

Solution: Phrase $36y^2$ can be written in form $(6y)^2$ and phrase $25x^4$ in form $(5x^2)^2$. Therefore, the relation of the question form is as follows:

$(6y)^2 - (5x^2)^2 = (6y - 5x^2)(6y + 5x^2)$.

Add Polynomials to Find Perimeter

- To find the perimeter of a two-dimensional shape whose sides are given as polynomials, the sum of polynomials is calculated.

Examples

Example 1. Find the perimeter. Simplify your answer.

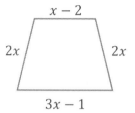

Solution: The perimeter of the shape is the sum of the sides. So,

$$\text{Perimeter} = (x - 2) + (2x) + (3x - 1) + (2x)$$

$$= x - 2 + 2x + 3x - 1 + 2x.$$

Group and add like terms,

$$\text{Perimeter} = (x + 2x + 3x + 2x) + (-2 - 1)$$

$$= 8x - 3.$$

Example 2. What is the perimeter of the rectangle if the length is $2x^2 - 1$ and the width is $4x + 2$?

Solution: The perimeter of the rectangle is,

$$\text{Perimeter} = 2\big((2x^2 - 1) + 4(x + 1)\big)$$

Expand the expression and simplify,

$$\text{Perimeter} = 2\big((2x^2 - 1) + (4x + 4)\big)$$

$$= 2(2x^2 - 1 + 4x + 4)$$

$$= 2(2x^2 + 4x + 3)$$

$$= 4x^2 + 8x + 6.$$

Find more at

bit.ly/3D5vQom

Chapter 11: Practices

✍ Simplify each polynomial.

1) $3(6x + 4) =$

2) $5(3x - 8) =$

3) $x(7x + 2) + 9x =$

4) $6x(x + 3) + 5x =$

5) $6x(3x + 1) - 5x =$

6) $x(3x - 4) + 3x^2 - 6 =$

7) $x^2 - 5 - 3x(x + 8) =$

8) $2x^2 + 7 - 6x(2x + 5) =$

✍ Add or subtract polynomials.

9) $(x^2 + 3) + (2x^2 - 4) =$

10) $(3x^2 - 6x) - (x^2 + 8x) =$

11) $(4x^3 - 3x^2) + (2x^3 - 5x^2) =$

12) $(6x^3 - 7x) - (5x^3 - 3x) =$

13) $(10x^3 + 4x^2) + (14x^2 - 8) =$

14) $(4x^3 - 9) - (3x^3 - 7x^2) =$

15) $(9x^3 + 3x) - (6x^3 - 4x) =$

16) $(7x^3 - 5x) - (3x^3 + 5x) =$

✍ Use algebra tiles to simplify polynomials.

17) $(2x^2 - 3x + 3) - (x^2 - x - 1)$

18) $(2x^2 + 2x + 5) + (x^2 + 2x + 1)$

✍ Find the products.

19) $3x^2 \times 8x^3 =$

20) $2x^4 \times 9x^3 =$

21) $-4a^4b \times 2ab^3 =$

22) $(-7x^3yz) \times (3xy^2z^4) =$

23) $-2a^5bc \times 6a^2b^4 =$

24) $9u^3t^2 \times (-2ut) =$

25) $12x^2z \times 3xy^3 =$

26) $11x^3z \times 5xy^5 =$

27) $-6a^3bc \times 5a^4b^3 =$

28) $-4x^6y^2 \times (-12xy) =$

✍ Simplify each expression.

29) $(7x^2y^3)(3x^4y^2) =$

30) $(6x^3y^2)(4x^4y^3) =$

31) $(10x^8y^5)(3x^5y^7) =$

32) $(15a^3b^2)(2a^3b^8) =$

33) $\frac{42x^4y^2}{6x^3y} =$

34) $\frac{49x^5y^6}{7x^2y} =$

35) $\frac{63x^{15}y^{10}}{9x^8y^6} =$

36) $\frac{35x^8y^{12}}{5x^4y^8} =$

✍ Find each product.

37) $3x(5x - y) =$

38) $2x(4x + y) =$

39) $7x(x - 3y) =$

40) $x(2x^2 + 2x - 4) =$

41) $5x(3x^2 + 8x + 2) =$

42) $7x(2x^2 - 9x - 5) =$

✍ Use the area model to find each product.

43) $3x(x + 2)$

44) $(a - 3)(2a + 2)$

✍ Find each product.

45) $(x - 3)(x + 3) =$

46) $(x - 6)(x + 6) =$

47) $(x + 10)(x + 4) =$

48) $(x - 6)(x + 7) =$

49) $(x + 2)(x - 5) =$

50) $(x - 10)(x + 3) =$

✎ Use algebra tiles to simplify.

51) $(x+1)(x+6)$ 52) $(2x+1)(x-4)$

✎ Factor each trinomial.

53) $x^2 + 6x + 8 =$ 56) $x^2 - 10x + 16 =$

54) $x^2 + 3x - 10 =$ 57) $2x^2 - 10x + 12 =$

55) $x^2 + 2x - 48 =$ 58) $3x^2 - 10x + 3 =$

✎ Factor each expression.

59) $4x^2 - 4x - 8$ 61) $16x^2 + 60x - 100$

60) $6x^2 + 37x + 6$ 62) $4x^2 - 17x + 4$

✎ Use a graph to factor the following polynomial.

63) $x^2 - 4$ 64) $-(x+2)^2$

✎ Factor each completely.

65) $36x^2 - 121$ 68) $49x^2 - 56x + 16 =$

66) $-36x^4 + 4x^2$ 69) $1 - x^2 =$

67) $-36x^2 + 400 =$ 70) $81x^4 - 900x^2 =$

✎ Find the perimeter.

71)

$3x + 6$

$(x + 2)$

72)

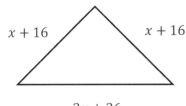

$x + 16$ $x + 16$

$2x + 36$

Chapter 11: Answers

1) $18x + 12$

2) $15x - 40$

3) $7x^2 + 11x$

4) $6x^2 + 23x$

5) $18x^2 + x$

6) $6x^2 - 4x - 6$

7) $-2x^2 - 24x - 5$

8) $-10x^2 - 30x + 7$

9) $3x^2 - 1$

10) $2x^2 - 14x$

11) $6x^3 - 8x^2$

12) $x^3 - 4x$

13) $10x^3 + 18x^2 - 8$

14) $x^3 + 7x^2 - 9$

15) $3x^3 + 7x$

16) $4x^3 - 10x$

17) $x^2 - 2x + 4$

18) $3x^2 + 4x + 6$

19) $24x^5$

20) $18x^7$

21) $-8a^5b^4$

22) $-21x^4y^3z^5$

23) $-12a^7b^5c$

24) $-18u^4t^3$

25) $36x^3y^3z$

26) $55x^4y^5z$

27) $-30a^7b^4c$

28) $48x^7y^3$

29) $21x^6y^5$

30) $24x^7y^5$

31) $30x^{13}y^{12}$

32) $30a^6b^{10}$

33) $7xy$

34) $7x^3y^5$

35) $7x^7y^4$

36) $7x^4y^4$

37) $15x^2 - 3xy$

38) $8x^2 + 2xy$

39) $7x^2 - 21xy$

40) $2x^3 + 2x^2 - 4x$

41) $15x^3 + 40x^2 + 10x$

42) $14x^3 - 63x^2 - 35x$

43) $3x^2 + 6x$

44) $2a^2 - 4a - 6$

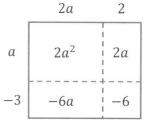

45) $x^2 - 9$

46) $x^2 - 36$

47) $x^2 + 14x + 40$

48) $x^2 + x - 42$

49) $x^2 - 3x - 10$

50) $x^2 - 7x - 30$

51) $x^2 + 7x + 6$

52) $2x^2 - 7x - 4$

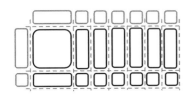

53) $(x + 4)(x + 2)$

54) $(x + 5)(x - 2)$

55) $(x - 6)(x + 8)$

56) $(x - 8)(x - 2)$

57) $(2x - 4)(x - 3)$

58) $(3x - 1)(x - 3)$

59) $4(x + 1)(x - 2)$

60) $(x + 6)(6x + 1)$

61) $4(x + 5)(4x - 5)$

62) $(x - 4)(4x - 1)$

63) $x = \pm 2$

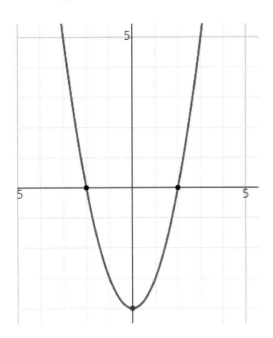

64) $x = -2$

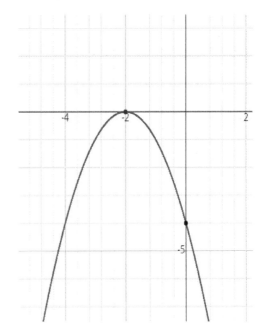

65) $(6x - 11)(6x + 11)$

66) $4x^2(1 - 3x)(1 + 3x)$

67) $4(10 + 3x)(10 - 3x)$

68) $(7x - 4)^2$

69) $(1 + x)(1 - x)$

70) $9x^2(3x + 10)(3x - 10)$

71) $8x + 16$

72) $4x + 68$

12 Relations and Functions

Math topics that you'll learn in this chapter:

- ☑ Function Notation and Evaluation
- ☑ Adding and Subtracting Functions
- ☑ Multiplying and Dividing Functions
- ☑ Composition of Functions
- ☑ Evaluate an Exponential Function
- ☑ Match Exponential Functions and Graphs
- ☑ Write Exponential Functions: Word Problems
- ☑ Function Inverses
- ☑ Domain and Range of Relations
- ☑ Rate of Change and Slope
- ☑ Complete a Function Table from an Equation

Function Notation and Evaluation

- Functions are mathematical operations that assign unique outputs to given inputs.

- Function notation is the way a function is written. It is meant to be a precise way of giving information about the function without a rather lengthy written explanation.

- The most popular function notation is $f(x)$ which is read "f of x". Any letter can name a function. For example: $g(x)$, $h(x)$, etc.

- To evaluate a function, plug in the input (the given value or expression) for the function's variable (place holder, x).

Examples:

Example 1. Evaluate: $f(x) = x + 6$, find $f(2)$

Solution: Substitute x with 2:

Then: $f(x) = x + 6 \rightarrow f(2) = 2 + 6 \rightarrow f(2) = 8$.

Example 2. Evaluate: $w(x) = 3x - 1$, find $w(4)$.

Solution: Substitute x with 4:

Then: $w(x) = 3x - 1 \rightarrow w(4) = 3(4) - 1 = 12 - 1 = 11$.

Example 3. Evaluate: $f(x) = 2x^2 + 4$, find $f(-1)$.

Solution: Substitute x with -1:

Then: $f(x) = 2x^2 + 4 \rightarrow f(-1) = 2(-1)^2 + 4 \rightarrow f(-1) = 2 + 4 = 6$.

Example 4. Evaluate: $h(x) = 4x^2 - 9$, find $h(2a)$.

Solution: Substitute x with $2a$:

Then: $h(x) = 4x^2 - 9 \rightarrow h(2a) = 4(2a)^2 - 9 \rightarrow h(2a) = 4(4a^2) - 9 = 16a^2 - 9$.

Adding and Subtracting Functions

- Just like we can add and subtract numbers and expressions, we can add or subtract functions and simplify or evaluate them. The result is a new function.

- For two functions $f(x)$ and $g(x)$, we can create two new functions:

$$(f + g)(x) = f(x) + g(x) \text{ and } (f - g)(x) = f(x) - g(x)$$

Examples:

Example 1. $g(x) = 2x - 2$, $f(x) = x + 1$, find: $(g + f)(x)$.

Solution: $(g + f)(x) = g(x) + f(x)$

Then: $(g + f)(x) = (2x - 2) + (x + 1) = 2x - 2 + x + 1 = 3x - 1$.

Example 2. $f(x) = 4x - 3$, $g(x) = 2x - 4$, find: $(f - g)(x)$.

Solution: $(f - g)(x) = f(x) - g(x)$

Then: $(f - g)(x) = (4x - 3) - (2x - 4) = 4x - 3 - 2x + 4 = 2x + 1$.

Example 3. $g(x) = x^2 + 2$, $f(x) = x + 5$, find: $(g + f)(x)$.

Solution: $(g + f)(x) = g(x) + f(x)$

Then: $(g + f)(x) = (x^2 + 2) + (x + 5) = x^2 + x + 7$.

Example 4. $f(x) = 5x^2 - 3$, $g(x) = 3x + 6$, find: $(f - g)(3)$.

Solution: $(f - g)(x) = f(x) - g(x)$

Then: $(f - g)(x) = (5x^2 - 3) - (3x + 6) = 5x^2 - 3 - 3x - 6 = 5x^2 - 3x - 9$.

Substitute x with 3: $(f - g)(3) = 5(3)^2 - 3(3) - 9 = 45 - 9 - 9 = 27$.

Example 5. $g(x) = x^2 - 4$, $f(x) = 2x + 3$, find: $(g + f)(x)$.

Solution: $(g + f)(x) = g(x) + f(x)$

Then: $(g + f)(x) = (x^2 - 4) + (2x + 3) = x^2 - 4 + 2x + 3 = x^2 + 2x - 1$.

bit.ly/3hdeFVO

Find more at

Multiplying and Dividing Functions

-   Just like we can multiply and divide numbers and expressions, we can multiply and divide two functions and simplify or evaluate them.

-   For two functions $f(x)$ and $g(x)$, we can create two new functions:

$$(f.g)(x) = f(x).g(x) \text{ and } \left(\frac{f}{g}\right)(x) = \frac{f(x)}{g(x)}$$

Examples:

Example 1. $g(x) = x + 3$, $f(x) = x + 4$, find: $(g.f)(x)$.

Solution:

$(g.f)(x) = g(x).f(x) = (x + 3)(x + 4) = x^2 + 4x + 3x + 12 = x^2 + 7x + 12$.

Example 2. $f(x) = x + 6$, $h(x) = x - 9$, find: $\left(\frac{f}{h}\right)(x)$.

Solution: $\left(\frac{f}{h}\right)(x) = \frac{f(x)}{h(x)} = \frac{x+6}{x-9}$.

Example 3. $g(x) = x + 7$, $f(x) = x - 3$, find: $(g.f)(2)$.

Solution: $(g.f)(x) = g(x).f(x) = (x + 7)(x - 3) = x^2 - 3x + 7x - 21$.

Then: $g(x).f(x) = x^2 + 4x - 21$.

Substitute x with 2: $(g.f)(2) = (2)^2 + 4(2) - 21 = 4 + 8 - 21 = -9$.

Example 4. $f(x) = x + 3$, $h(x) = 2x - 4$, find: $\left(\frac{f}{h}\right)(3)$.

Solution: $\left(\frac{f}{h}\right)(x) = \frac{f(x)}{h(x)} = \frac{x+3}{2x-4}$.

Substitute x with 3: $\left(\frac{f}{h}\right)(3) = \frac{3+3}{2(3)-4} = \frac{6}{2} = 3$.

Example 5. $g(x) = x + 5$, $f(x) = x - 2$, find: $(g.f)(4)$.

Solution: $(g.f)(x) = g(x).f(x) = (x + 5)(x - 2) = x^2 + 3x - 10$.

Substitute x with 4: $(g.f)(4) = (4)^2 + 3(4) - 10 = 16 + 12 - 10 = 18$.

Composition of Functions

- "Composition of functions" simply means combining two or more functions in a way where the output from one function becomes the input for the next function.

- The notation used for a composition is: $(fog)(x) = f\big(g(x)\big)$ and is read

  "f composed with g of x" or "f of g of x".

Examples:

Example 1. Using $f(x) = 2x + 3$ and $g(x) = 5x$, find: $(fog)(x)$.

Solution: $(fog)(x) = f\big(g(x)\big)$. Then:
$$(fog)(x) = f\big(g(x)\big) = f(5x).$$
Now find $f(5x)$ by substituting x with $5x$ in $f(x)$ function.
Then:
$$f(x) = 2x + 3; (x \to 5x) \to f(5x) = 2(5x) + 3 = 10x + 3.$$

Example 2. Using $f(x) = 3x - 1$ and $g(x) = 2x - 2$, find: $(gof)(5)$.

Solution: $(fog)(x) = f\big(g(x)\big)$. Then:
$$(gof)(x) = g\big(f(x)\big) = g(3x - 1),$$
Now substitute x in $g(x)$ by $(3x - 1)$.
Then:
$$g(3x - 1) = 2(3x - 1) - 2 = 6x - 2 - 2 = 6x - 4.$$
Substitute x with 5: $(gof)(5) = g\big(f(5)\big) = 6(5) - 4 = 30 - 4 = 26.$

Example 3. Using $f(x) = 2x^2 - 5$ and $g(x) = x + 3$, find: $f\big(g(3)\big)$.

Solution: First, find $g(3)$:
$$g(x) = x + 3 \to g(3) = 3 + 3 = 6.$$
Then: $f\big(g(3)\big) = f(6)$.
Now, find $f(6)$ by substituting x with 6 in $f(x)$ function.
$$f\big(g(3)\big) = f(6) = 2(6)^2 - 5 = 2(36) - 5 = 67.$$

bit.ly/2WHBkAg
Find more at

Evaluate an Exponential Function

- For any real number x, an exponential function is an equation with the form $f(x) = ab^x$, where a is a non-zero real number and b is a positive real number.

- To evaluate the value of an exponential function, it's enough to substitute the given input for the independent variable.

Examples:

Example 1. Let $f(x) = 3^x$. What is $f(2)$?

Solution: To solve, it is enough to substitute $x = 2$, in the equation $f(x) = 3^x$. So, $f(2) = 3^2 = 9$.

Example 2. Let $f(x) = 7(2)^x$. Evaluate $f(3)$.

Solution: To evaluate $f(3)$, plug 3 in equation $f(x) = 7(2)^x$ instead of the independent variable x. Therefore,

$$f(3) = 7(2)^3 = 7(8) = 56.$$

Example 3. Use the following function to find $f(6)$.

$$f(x) = -2(3)^{\frac{x}{2}-1}$$

Solution: First, substitute $x = 6$ in the equation,

$$f(6) = -2(3)^{\frac{6}{2}-1} = -2(3)^{3-1} = -2(3)^2 = -2(9) = -18.$$

Example 4. Use the following function to find $f(2)$.

$$f(x) = 9\left(\frac{1}{3}\right)^{2x-1} + 1$$

Solution: To solve, plug 2 into $f(x) = 9\left(\frac{1}{3}\right)^{2x-1} + 1$ instead of x. So,

$$f(2) = 9\left(\frac{1}{3}\right)^{2(2)-1} + 1 = 9\left(\frac{1}{3}\right)^{2(2)-1} + 1 = 9\left(\frac{1}{3}\right)^{4-1} + 1 = 9\left(\frac{1}{3}\right)^3 + 1$$

$$= 9\left(\frac{1}{27}\right) + 1 = \frac{1}{3} + 1 = \frac{4}{3}.$$

Match Exponential Functions and Graphs

- To match an exponential function $y = b^x$ with its graph and vice versa, use points to identify the important parameters of the graph of an exponential function, which are:
- Look for the relationship as growth or decay. By checking:
  - If $b > 1$, the function is growing.
  - If $0 < b < 1$, the function is decaying.
- Evaluate the value of the function at a few inputs to match some points on the graph, like the $y-$intercept.
- Determine the end behavior of the function.

Example:

Match each exponential function to its graph.

$$f(x) = \left(\frac{1}{2}\right)^x, g(x) = \left(\frac{3}{2}\right)^x, h(x) = \left(\frac{1}{3}\right)^x$$

A

B

C

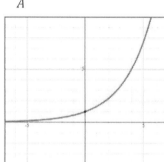 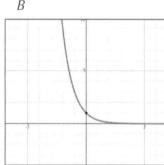 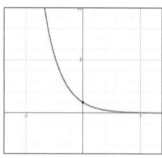

Solution: According to the base value of the exponential equation, notice that one of the functions is growing and the other two functions are decaying. So, the function $g(x) = \left(\frac{3}{2}\right)^x$ can be equivalent to graph A. Now, evaluate the two remaining functions at a few inputs to find some points on the graph. Choose a point such as -1 to plug into the equation. Therefore, start with $f(x) = \left(\frac{1}{2}\right)^x$.

$$f(-1) = \left(\frac{1}{2}\right)^{-1} = 2.$$

You can see that the ordered pair $(-1,2)$ for the function $f(x) = \left(\frac{1}{2}\right)^x$ is equivalent to a point on graph C. In the same way, substitute -1 in $h(x) = \left(\frac{1}{3}\right)^x$. Therefore, $h(-1) = \left(\frac{1}{3}\right)^{-1} = 3$. That is, graph B represented the function $h(x)$.

Write Exponential Functions: Word Problems

- To solve the word problems corresponding to the exponential function, follow the steps which are:

Step 1: Check that it changes at the constant ratio.

Step 2: Identify the given values such as the ratio and the initial amount.

Step 3: Substitute in the exponential formula.

Step 4: Evaluate the requested values.

Examples:

Example 1. In a laboratory sample, if it starts with 100 bacteria which can double every hour, how many bacteria will there be after 6 hours?

Solution: Since it grows at the constant ratio of 2, you have to use the formula of exponential to find the number of bacteria in this sample. Use the formula,

$$y = ab^n$$

Where $a = 100$ is the initial number of bacteria, and b is equal to 2. Substitute the given value in the formula, then:

$$y = 100(2)^n$$

Now, plug $n = 6$ into the equation. Therefore, $y = 100(2)^6 = 100(64) = 6,400$.

Example 2. Mrs. Shelby's new car cost \$12,000. It depreciates in value by about 10% each year. Write an equation that would indicate the value of the car at the tth year. How much will her car be worth in 8 years?

Solution: To write the equation of the value of the car at the tth year, use the formula given as follow: $y = ab^x$, where a is the initial amount, and b is the ratio of changes. The initial cost of the car is \$12,000. So, the equation is

$$y = 12,000(0.9)^t$$

Now, plug $t = 8$ in $y = 12,000(0.9)^t$. Therefore,

$$y = 12,000(0.9)^8$$

$$\cong 12,000(0.43) = 5,160.$$

bit.ly/3HjClGF

Find more at

Function Inverses

- An inverse function is a function that reverses another function: if the function f applied to an input x gives a result of y, then applying its inverse function g to y gives the result x.

- $f(x) = y$ if and only if $g(y) = x$.

- The inverse function of $f(x)$ is usually shown by $f^{-1}(x)$.

Examples:

Example 1. Find the inverse of the function: $f(x) = 2x - 1$.

Solution: First, replace $f(x)$ with y: $y = 2x - 1$. Then, replace all x's with y and all y's with x: $x = 2y - 1$.

Now, solve for y: $x = 2y - 1 \rightarrow x + 1 = 2y \rightarrow \frac{1}{2}x + \frac{1}{2} = y$.

Finally replace y with $f^{-1}(x)$:

$$f^{-1}(x) = \frac{1}{2}x + \frac{1}{2}.$$

Example 2. Find the inverse of the function: $g(x) = \frac{1}{5}x + 3$.

Solution: $g(x) = \frac{1}{5}x + 3 \rightarrow y = \frac{1}{5}x + 3$,

replace all x's with y and all y's with x; $x = \frac{1}{5}y + 3$,

solve for y:

$$x - 3 = \frac{1}{5}y \rightarrow 5(x - 3) = y \rightarrow g^{-1}(x) = 5x - 15.$$

Example 3. Find the inverse of the function: $h(x) = \sqrt{x} + 6$.

Solution: $h(x) = \sqrt{x} + 6 \rightarrow y = \sqrt{x} + 6$,

replace all x's with y and all y's with x;

$$x = \sqrt{y} + 6 \rightarrow x - 6 = \sqrt{y} \rightarrow (x - 6)^2 = (\sqrt{y})^2 \rightarrow x^2 - 12x + 36 = y.$$

Then:

$$h^{-1}(x) = x^2 - 12x + 36.$$

Domain and Range of Relations

- A relation is defined as a set or the desired set's connection. An ordered pair commonly is named a point, and a relation is a set of these ordered pairs. In fact, input and output values in a relationship are shown in ordered pairs. In other words, a relation is a kind of rule that connects a component or value from one set to a component or value from the other set.

- The domain refers to all of the input or independent values that are put into a relation or a function. The range refers to all of the output or dependent values that leave from a relation or a function.

- A function is a group of ordered pairs that each input element just is related to an output element. In other words, in a function 2 input values can be connected to the same output value but it's not possible that 2 output values are connected to the same input value.

- When you have a graph, the $x-$coordinates of the graph are domain and the $y-$coordinates of the graph are range. The $x-$coordinates are the domain value, when you put them into the function, the output values you have found will be placed on the $y-$axis.

Examples:

Example 1. What is the domain and range of the following relation: $\{(7,2), (-3,4), (4,-1), (5,3), (8,5)\}$?

Solution: The domain contains $x-$values of a relation and the range includes $y-$values of a relationship. So, Domain $= \{7, -3, 4, 5, 8\}$ and Range $= \{2, 4, -1, 3, 5\}$.

Example 2. Find the domain and range of the following relation:
$R = \{(4x + 1, x - 2): x \in \{-2, -1, 0, 2, 3\}$

Solution: Given the relation $R = \{4x + 1, x - 2\}$ where x belongs to the set $\{-2, -1, 0, 2, 3\}$, let's determine the output values for each value of x. For $x = -2$: $4(-2) + 1 = -7, (-2) - 2 = -4$. For $x = -1$: $4(-1) + 1 = -3, (-1) - 2 = -3$. For $x = 0$: $4(0) + 1 = 1, 0 - 2 = -2$. For $x = 2$: $4(2) + 1 = 9, 2 - 2 = 0$. For $x = 3$: $4(3) + 1 = 13, 3 - 2 = 1$.

From the calculations we have: $R = \{(-7, -4), (-3, -3), (1, -2), (9, 0), (13, 1)\}$

Domain $= \{-7, -3, 1, 9, 13\}$.

Range $= \{-4, -3, -2, 0, 1\}$,

bit.ly/3R4PhDK

Find more at

Rate of Change and Slope

- A ratio that uses to compare the change in y −values to the change in the x −values is called the rate of change. y −values are considered as the dependent variables and x −values are considered as the independent variables. The rate of change is the line's slope when the rate of change is constant and linear. The line's slope can be negative, positive, zero, or undefined.

- The direction of a line's slope can also describe a slope of a line. If a line is a rising line from left to right its slope is positive. If a line is a falling line from left to right, its slope is negative. In the case when you have a horizontal line it means that no change happens, so the slope of the line is zero. when you have a vertical line, this relationship is not a function, and the slope is undefined. It's because there are many y −values for one x −value.

- The variable m is the sign for the slope of a line. It is stated by the ratio of the subtraction of y −variables to the subtraction of x −variables. It means if $(x_1, y_1)(x_2, y_2)$ are the coordinates of 2 points on a line, then $m = \frac{y_2 - y_1}{x_2 - x_1}$.

Example:

The following table shows the number of cars sold by a company in different years. Find the rate of change in car sales for each time interval. Determine which time interval has the greatest rate.

Year	2005	2010	2015	2020	2022
Number of sold cars	35	45	47	67	85

Solution: First, find the dependent and independent variables: years are independent variables and the number of sold cars are dependent variables.

Now find the rate of changes: 2005 to 2010 $\rightarrow \frac{change\ in\ the\ number\ of\ sold\ cars}{change\ in\ years} =$

$\frac{45-35}{2010-2005} = 2.$ 2010 to 2015 $\rightarrow \frac{change\ in\ the\ number\ of\ sold\ cars}{change\ in\ years} = \frac{47-45}{2015-2010} = 0.4.$ 2015 to

2020 $\rightarrow \frac{change\ in\ the\ number\ of\ sold\ cars}{change\ in\ years} = \frac{67-47}{2020-2015} = 4.$ 2022 to 2020 $\rightarrow$

$\frac{change\ in\ the\ number\ of\ sold\ cars}{change\ in\ years} = \frac{85-67}{2022-2020} = 9.$ Car sales have been at their greatest

rate from 2022 to 2020. The slope of the line is positive because as the time period increases, the amount of car sales also increases.

bit.ly/3IruGqT

Find more at

Complete a Function Table from an Equation

- One of the main ways to show a relationship in mathematics is by using a function table.

- To complete a function table of the given equation:

  Step 1: Consider the input and output in the table.

  Step 2: Substitute the given value for the input.

  Step 3: Evaluate the output of the equation.

Example:

Complete the table.

$f(x) = 2x - 1$	
x	$f(x)$
-2	
0	
1	

Solution: Look at the function table. Clearly, the first value of the input in the table

is -2. Evaluate $f(x) = 2x - 1$ for $x = -2$.

$$f(-2) = 2(-2) - 1$$

$$= -4 - 1 = -5.$$

$f(x) = 2x - 1$	
x	$f(x)$
-2	-5
0	
1	

When $x = -2$, then $f(-2) = -5$. Complete the first row of the table.

Similarly, evaluate $f(x) = 2x - 1$ for $x = 0$ and $x = 1$, respectively. So,

$$f(0) = 2(0) - 1 = 0 - 1 = -1,$$

$$f(1) = 2(1) - 1 = 2 - 1 = 1.$$

Enter the obtained values in the table.

$f(x) = 2x - 1$	
x	$f(x)$
-2	-5
0	-1
1	1

Chapter 12: Practices

✍ Evaluate each function.

1) $f(x) = x - 2$, find $f(-1)$

2) $g(x) = 2x + 4$, find $g(3)$

3) $g(n) = 2n - 8$, find $g(-1)$

4) $h(n) = n^2 - 1$, find $h(-2)$

5) $f(x) = x^2 + 12$, find $f(5)$

6) $g(x) = 2x^2 - 9$, find $g(-2)$

7) $w(x) = 2x^2 - 4x$, find $w(2n)$

8) $p(x) = 4x^3 - 10$, find $p(-3a)$

✍ Perform the indicated operation.

9) $g(x) = x - 2$
$h(x) = 2x + 6$
Find: $(h + g)(3)$

_____

10) $f(x) = 3x + 2$
$g(x) = -x - 6$
Find: $(f + g)(2)$

_____

11) $f(x) = 5x + 8$
$g(x) = 3x - 12$
Find: $(f - g)(-2)$

_____

12) $h(x) = 2x^2 - 10$
$g(x) = 3x + 12$
Find: $(h + g)(3)$

_____

13) $g(x) = 12x - 8$
$h(x) = 3x^2 + 14$
Find: $(h - g)(x)$

_____

14) $h(x) = -2x^2 - 18$
$g(x) = 4x^2 + 15$
Find: $(h - g)(a)$

_____

✍ Perform the indicated operation.

15) $g(x) = x - 5$
$h(x) = x + 6$
Find: $(g.h)(-1)$

_____

16) $f(x) = 2x + 2$
$g(x) = -x - 6$
Find: $(\frac{f}{g})(-2)$

_____

17) $f(x) = 5x + 3$
$g(x) = 2x - 4$
Find: $(\frac{f}{g})(5)$

_____

18) $h(x) = x^2 - 2$
$g(x) = x + 4$
Find: $(g.h)(3)$

_____

19) $g(x) = 4x - 12$
$h(x) = x^2 + 4$
Find: $(g.h)(-2)$

_____

20) $h(x) = 3x^2 - 8$
$g(x) = 4x + 6$
Find: $(\frac{h}{g})(-4)$

_____

✐ Solve.

21) $f(x) = 2x$

    $g(x) = x + 3$

    Find: $(fog)(2)$

    _____

22) $f(x) = x + 2$

    $g(x) = x - 6$

    Find: $(fog)(-1)$

    _____

23) $f(x) = 3x$

    $g(x) = x + 4$

    Find: $(gof)(4)$

    _____

24) $h(x) = 2x - 2$

    $g(x) = x + 4$

    Find: $(goh)(2)$

    _____

25) $f(x) = 2x - 8$

    $g(x) = x + 10$

    Find: $(fog)(-2)$

    _____

26) $f(x) = x^2 - 8$

    $g(x) = 2x + 3$

    Find: $(gof)(4)$

    _____

✐ Use the following function to find: $f(x) = 3x\left(\frac{1}{2}\right)^{2x+2}$

27) $f(2)$

28) $f(4)$

✐ Match each exponential function to its graph.

29) $f(x) = -4(3)^x$, $f(x) = 2^x + 5$, $f(x) = 3(2)^x + 3$

        A   B   C

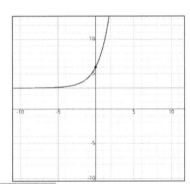
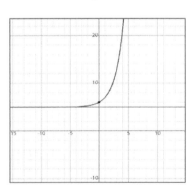
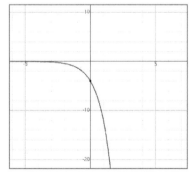

✍ **Solve.**

30) As of 2019, the world population is 8.716 billion and growing at a rate of 1.2% per year. Write an equation to model population growth, where $p(t)$ is the population in billions of people and t is the time in years.

31) You decide to buy a used car that costs \$20,000. You have heard that the car may depreciate at a rate of 10% per year. At this rate, how much will the car be worth in 6 years?

✍ **Find the inverse of each function.**

32) $f(x) = -\frac{1}{x} - 9$

$f^{-1}(x) =$ _____

33) $g(x) = \sqrt{x} - 2$

$g^{-1}(x) =$ _____

34) $h(x) = -\frac{5}{x+3}$

$h^{-1}(x) =$ _____

35) $f(x) = 6x + 6$

$f^{-1}(x) =$ _____

✍ **Find the domain and range of each relation.**

36) $\{(1, -1), (2, -4), (0,5), (-1,6)\}$

37) $\{(10, -5), (-16, -8), (-4, 19), (16, 7), (6, -14)\}$

38) $\{(4, 7), (-15, 6), (-20, 9), (13, 8), (7, 5)\}$

✍ **Solve.**

39) Average food preparation time in a restaurant was tracked daily as part of an efficiency improvement program.

Day	Food preparation time (minutes)
Tuesday	45
Wednesday	49
Thursday	32
Friday	15
Saturday	25

According to the table, what was the rate of change between Tuesday and Wednesday?

✍ Complete the table.

40)

$f(x) = 3x - 2$	
x	$f(x)$
-3	
0	
2	

41)

$f(x) = 2x$	
x	$f(x)$
1	
2	
3	

Chapter 12: Answers

1) -3

2) 10

3) -10

4) 3

5) 37

6) -1

7) $8n^2 - 8n$

8) $-108a^3 - 10$

9) 13

10) 0

11) 16

12) 29

13) $3x^2 - 12x + 22$

14) $-6a^2 - 33$

15) -30

16) $\frac{1}{2}$

17) $\frac{14}{3}$

18) 49

19) -160

20) -4

21) 10

22) -5

23) 16

24) 6

25) 8

26) 19

27) $\frac{3}{32}$

28) $\frac{3}{256}$

29) $A = 3(2)^x + 3,$

$B = 2^x + 5,$

$C = -4(3)^x$

30) $p(t) = 8.716(1 + 0.012)^t$

31) $A = 20,000(1 - 0.1)^6$

32) $-\frac{1}{x+9}$

33) $x^2 + 4x + 4$

34) $-\frac{5}{x} - 3$

35) $\frac{x-6}{6}$

36) $D = (1,2,0,-1),$

   $R = (-1,-4,5,6)$

37) $D = (10,-16,-4,16,6),$

   $R = (-5,-8,19,7,-14)$

38) $D = (4,-15,-20,13,7),$

   $R = (7,6,9,8,5)$

39) 4

40)

$f(x) = 3x - 2$	
x	$f(x)$
-3	-11
0	-2
2	4

41)

$f(x) = 2x$	
x	$f(x)$
1	2
2	4
3	6

CHAPTER

13 Radical Expressions

Math topics that you'll learn in this chapter:

- ☑ Simplifying Radical Expressions
- ☑ Adding and Subtracting Radical Expressions
- ☑ Multiplying Radical Expressions
- ☑ Rationalizing Radical Expressions
- ☑ Radical Equations
- ☑ Domain and Range of Radical Functions
- ☑ Simplify Radicals with Fractions

161

Simplifying Radical Expressions

- Find the prime factors of the numbers or expressions inside the radical.

- Use radical properties to simplify the radical expression:

$$\sqrt[n]{x^a} = x^{\frac{a}{n}}, \quad \sqrt[n]{xy} = x^{\frac{1}{n}} \times y^{\frac{1}{n}}, \quad \sqrt[n]{\frac{x}{y}} = \frac{x^{\frac{1}{n}}}{y^{\frac{1}{n}}}, \text{ and } \sqrt[n]{x} \times \sqrt[n]{y} = \sqrt[n]{xy}$$

Examples:

Example 1. Find the square root of $\sqrt{144x^2}$.

Solution: Find the factor of the expression $144x^2$: $144 = 12 \times 12$ and

$x^2 = x \times x$, now use radical rule: $\sqrt[n]{a^n} = a$.

Then: $\sqrt{12^2} = 12$ and $\sqrt{x^2} = x$.

Finally:

$$\sqrt{144x^2} = \sqrt{12^2} \times \sqrt{x^2} = 12 \times x = 12x.$$

Example 2. Write this radical in exponential form. $\sqrt[3]{x^4}$

Solution: To write a radical in exponential form, use this rule: $\sqrt[n]{x^a} = x^{\frac{a}{n}}$.

Then:

$$\sqrt[3]{x^4} = x^{\frac{4}{3}}.$$

Example 3. Simplify. $\sqrt{8x^3}$

Solution: First factor the expression $8x^3$: $8x^3 = 2^3 \times x \times x \times x$, we need to find perfect

squares: $8x^3 = 2^2 \times 2 \times x^2 \times x = 2^2 \times x^2 \times 2x,$

Then:

$$\sqrt{8x^3} = \sqrt{2^2 \times x^2} \times \sqrt{2x}.$$

Now use radical rule: $\sqrt[n]{a^n} = a$.

Then:

$$\sqrt{2^2 \times x^2} \times \sqrt{(2x)} = 2x \times \sqrt{2x} = 2x\sqrt{2x}.$$

bit.ly/3fbGZJm

Find more at

Adding and Subtracting Radical Expressions

- Only numbers and expressions that have the same radical part can be added or subtracted.

- Remember, combining "unlike" radical terms is not possible.

- For numbers with the same radical part, just add or subtract factors outside the radicals.

Examples:

Example 1. Simplify: $6\sqrt{2} + 5\sqrt{2}$.

Solution: Since we have the same radical parts, then we can add these two radicals. Add like terms:

$$6\sqrt{2} + 5\sqrt{2} = 11\sqrt{2}.$$

Example 2. Simplify: $2\sqrt{8} - 2\sqrt{2}$.

Solution: The two radical parts are not the same. First, we need to simplify the $2\sqrt{8}$. Then:

$$2\sqrt{8} = 2\sqrt{4 \times 2} = 2(\sqrt{4})(\sqrt{2}) = 4\sqrt{2}.$$

Now, combine like terms:

$$2\sqrt{8} - 2\sqrt{2} = 4\sqrt{2} - 2\sqrt{2} = 2\sqrt{2}.$$

Example 3. Simplify: $8\sqrt{27} + 5\sqrt{3}$.

Solution: The two radical parts are not the same. First, we need to simplify the $8\sqrt{27}$. Then:

$$8\sqrt{27} = 8\sqrt{9 \times 3} = 8(\sqrt{9})(\sqrt{3}) = 24\sqrt{3}.$$

Now, add:

$$8\sqrt{27} + 5\sqrt{3} = 24\sqrt{3} + 5\sqrt{3} = 29\sqrt{3}.$$

bit.ly/2PkJfTA
Find more at

Multiplying Radical Expressions

To multiply radical expressions:

- Multiply the numbers and expressions outside of the radicals.

- Multiply the numbers and expressions inside the radicals.

- Simplify if needed.

Examples:

Example 1. Evaluate. $2\sqrt{5} \times \sqrt{3}$

Solution: Multiply the numbers outside of the radicals and the radical parts. Then:

$$2\sqrt{5} \times \sqrt{3} = (2 \times 1) \times (\sqrt{5} \times \sqrt{3}) = 2\sqrt{15}.$$

Example 2. Simplify. $3x\sqrt{3} \times 4\sqrt{x}$

Solution: Multiply the numbers outside of the radicals and the radical parts. Then, simplify:

$$3x\sqrt{3} \times 4\sqrt{x} = (3x \times 4) \times (\sqrt{3} \times \sqrt{x}) = (12x)(\sqrt{3x}) = 12x\sqrt{3x}.$$

Example 3. Evaluate. $6a\sqrt{7b} \times 3\sqrt{2b}$

Solution: Multiply the numbers outside of the radicals and the radical parts. Then:

$$6a\sqrt{7b} \times 3\sqrt{2b} = 6a \times 3 \times \sqrt{7b} \times \sqrt{2b} = 18a\sqrt{14b^2}.$$

Simplify:

$$18a\sqrt{14b^2} = 18a \times \sqrt{14} \times \sqrt{b^2} = 18ab\sqrt{14}.$$

Example 4. Simplify. $9\sqrt{9x} \times 5\sqrt{4x}$

Solution: Multiply the numbers outside of the radicals and the radical parts. Then, simplify: $9\sqrt{9x} \times 5\sqrt{4x} = (9 \times 5) \times (\sqrt{9x} \times \sqrt{4x}) = (45)(\sqrt{36x^2}) = 45\sqrt{36x^2}.$

$\sqrt{36x^2} = 6x$, then:

$$45\sqrt{36x^2} = 45 \times 6x = 270x.$$

bit.ly/3ri1RqN

Find more at

Rationalizing Radical Expressions

- Radical expressions cannot be in the denominator. (Number in the bottom)

- To get rid of the radical in the denominator, multiply both the numerator and denominator by the radical in the denominator.

- If there is a radical and another integer in the denominator, multiply both the numerator and denominator by the conjugate of the denominator.

- The conjugate of $(a + b)$ is $(a - b)$ and vice versa.

Examples:

Example 1. Simplify: $\frac{9}{\sqrt{3}}$.

Solution: Multiply both the numerator and denominator by $\sqrt{3}$. Then:

$$\frac{9}{\sqrt{3}} \times \frac{\sqrt{3}}{\sqrt{3}} = \frac{9\sqrt{3}}{\sqrt{9}} = \frac{9\sqrt{3}}{3}.$$

Now, simplify: $\frac{9\sqrt{3}}{3} = 3\sqrt{3}$.

Example 2. Simplify $\frac{5}{\sqrt{6}-4}$.

Solution: Multiply by the conjugate: $\frac{\sqrt{6}+4}{\sqrt{6}+4} \rightarrow \frac{5}{\sqrt{6}-4} \times \frac{\sqrt{6}+4}{\sqrt{6}+4}$.

$$\left(\sqrt{6} - 4\right)\left(\sqrt{6} + 4\right) = -10,$$

then: $\frac{5}{\sqrt{6}-4} \times \frac{\sqrt{6}+4}{\sqrt{6}+4} = \frac{5\left(\sqrt{6}+4\right)}{-10}$.

Use the fraction rule:

$$\frac{a}{-b} = -\frac{a}{b} \rightarrow \frac{5\left(\sqrt{6}+4\right)}{-10} = -\frac{5\left(\sqrt{6}+4\right)}{10} = -\frac{1}{2}\left(\sqrt{6} + 4\right).$$

Example 3. Simplify $\frac{2}{\sqrt{3}-1}$.

Solution: Multiply by the conjugate: $\frac{\sqrt{3}+1}{\sqrt{3}+1}$.

$$\frac{2}{\sqrt{3}-1} \times \frac{\sqrt{3}+1}{\sqrt{3}+1} = \frac{2\left(\sqrt{3}+1\right)}{2} = \left(\sqrt{3} + 1\right).$$

bit.ly/3vKudGO

Find more at

Radical Equations

- Isolate the radical on one side of the equation.

- Square both sides of the equation to remove the radical.

- Solve the equation for the variable.

- Plugin the answer (answers) into the original equation to avoid extraneous values.

Examples:

Example 1. Solve $\sqrt{x} - 5 = 15$.

Solution: Add 5 to both sides:

$$\left(\sqrt{x} - 5\right) + 5 = 15 + 5 \rightarrow \sqrt{x} = 20,$$

square both sides:

$$\left(\sqrt{x}\right)^2 = 20^2 \rightarrow x = 400.$$

Plugin the value of 400 for x in the original equation and check the answer:

$$x = 400 \rightarrow \sqrt{x} - 5 = \sqrt{400} - 5 = 20 - 5 = 15,$$

so, the value of 400 for x is correct.

Example 2. What is the value of x in this equation? $2\sqrt{x + 1} = 4$

Solution: Divide both sides by 2. Then:

$$2\sqrt{x + 1} = 4 \rightarrow \frac{2\sqrt{x+1}}{2} = \frac{4}{2} \rightarrow \sqrt{x + 1} = 2.$$

Square both sides: $\left(\sqrt{(x + 1)}\right)^2 = 2^2.$

Then $x + 1 = 4 \rightarrow x = 3.$

Substitute x by 3 in the original equation and check the answer:

$$x = 3 \rightarrow 2\sqrt{x + 1} = 2\sqrt{3 + 1} = 2\sqrt{4} = 2(2) = 4.$$

So, the value of 3 for x is correct.

Domain and Range of Radical Functions

- To find the domain of the function, find all possible values of the variable inside the radical.

- Remember that having a negative number under the square root symbol is not possible. (For cubic roots, we can have negative numbers.)

- To find the range, plugin the minimum and maximum values of the variable inside radical.

Examples:

Example 1. Find the domain and range of the radical function.

$$y = \sqrt{x - 3}$$

Solution: For domain: find non-negative values for radicals: $x - 3 \geq 0$.

Domain of functions: $\sqrt{f(x)} \rightarrow f(x) \geq 0$, then solve $x - 3 \geq 0 \rightarrow x \geq 3$.

Domain of the function $y = \sqrt{x - 3}$: $x \geq 3$.

For range: the range of a radical function of the form $c\sqrt{ax + b} + k$ is:

$$f(x) \geq k$$

For the function $y = \sqrt{x - 3}$, the value of k is 0. Then: $f(x) \geq 0$.

Range of the function $y = \sqrt{x - 3}$: $f(x) \geq 0$.

Example 2. Find the domain and range of the radical function.

$$y = 6\sqrt{4x + 8} + 5$$

Solution: For domain: find non-negative values for radicals: $4x + 8 \geq 0$.

Domain of functions: $4x + 8 \geq 0 \rightarrow 4x \geq -8 \rightarrow x \geq -2$.

Domain of the function $y = 6\sqrt{4x + 8} + 5$: $x \geq -2$.

For range: the range of a radical function of the form $c\sqrt{ax + b} + k$ is: $f(x) \geq k$.

For the function $y = 6\sqrt{4x + 8} + 5$, the value of k is 5. Then: $f(x) \geq 5$.

Range of the function $y = 6\sqrt{4x + 8} + 5$: $f(x) \geq 5$.

bit.ly/2Pn4vIj

Find more at

Simplify Radicals with Fractions

- To simplify radicals with fractions:
  - Rewrite the numerator and denominator of the fraction as the product of the prime factorizations.
  - Apply the multiplication and division properties of radical expressions.
  - Group the factors that form a perfect square, perfect cube and etc.
  - Simplify.

Examples:

Example 1. Simplify. $\sqrt{\frac{9}{25}}$

Solution: To simplify the radical fraction, rewrite the numerator and denominator as the product of the prime factorizations. So, $\sqrt{\frac{9}{25}} = \sqrt{\frac{3 \times 3}{5 \times 5}}$.

Since the index of the given radical is 2. You can take one term out of radical for every two same terms multiplied inside the radical sign (perfect square). Then: $\sqrt{\frac{3 \times 3}{5 \times 5}} = \frac{3}{5}$.

Example 2. Simplify the following radical fraction: $\sqrt{\frac{44}{16}}$.

Solution: Rewrite the numerator and denominator of the fraction as follows: $\sqrt{\frac{44}{16}} = \sqrt{\frac{2 \times 2 \times 11}{2 \times 2 \times 2 \times 2}}$. Consider the index of the given radical, take out one term of radical for every term that is repeated in an even number inside the radical sign. So, $\sqrt{\frac{2 \times 2 \times 11}{2 \times 2 \times 2 \times 2}} = \frac{2\sqrt{11}}{4}$. Simplify, $\frac{2\sqrt{11}}{4} = \frac{\sqrt{11}}{2}$.

Example 3. Write the expression in the simplest radical form. $\sqrt{\frac{242}{45}}$

Solution: Rewrite this radical fraction as the product of the prime factorizations: $\sqrt{\frac{242}{45}} = \sqrt{\frac{2 \times 11 \times 11}{3 \times 3 \times 5}}$. Now, take out the terms that are perfect squares, so, $\sqrt{\frac{2 \times 11 \times 11}{3 \times 3 \times 5}} = \frac{11}{3}\sqrt{\frac{2}{5}}$.

Chapter 13: Practices

✒ Evaluate.

1) $\sqrt{49} = $ _____

2) $\sqrt{4} \times \sqrt{81} = $ _____

3) $\sqrt{16} \times \sqrt{4x^2} = $ _____

4) $\sqrt{289} = $ _____

5) $\sqrt{25b^4} = $ _____

6) $\sqrt{9} \times \sqrt{x^2} = $ _____

✒ Simplify.

7) $\sqrt{6} + 6\sqrt{6} = $

8) $9\sqrt{8} - 6\sqrt{2} = $

9) $-\sqrt{7} - 5\sqrt{7} = $

10) $10\sqrt{2} + 3\sqrt{18} = $

11) $\sqrt{12} - 6\sqrt{3} = $

12) $-2\sqrt{x} + 6\sqrt{x} = $

✒ Evaluate.

13) $\sqrt{4} \times 2\sqrt{9} = $

14) $\sqrt{5} \times 3\sqrt{20y} = $

15) $-6\sqrt{4} \times 3\sqrt{4} = $

16) $-9\sqrt{3b^2} \times (-\sqrt{6}) = $

✒ Simplify.

17) $\frac{1+\sqrt{5}}{1-\sqrt{3}} = $

18) $\frac{2+\sqrt{6}}{\sqrt{2}-\sqrt{5}} = $

19) $\frac{\sqrt{7}}{\sqrt{6}-\sqrt{3}} = $

20) $\frac{\sqrt{8a}}{\sqrt{a^5}} = $

✒ Solve for x in each equation.

21) $2\sqrt{2x-4} = 8$

22) $9 = \sqrt{4x-1}$

23) $\sqrt{x} + 6 = 11$

24) $\sqrt{5x} = \sqrt{x+3}$

bit.ly/3RAbyde

Solutions at

✒ Identify the domain and range of each function.

25) $y = \sqrt{x + 1}$

26) $y = \sqrt{x - 2} + 6$

27) $y = \sqrt{x} - 1$

28) $y = \sqrt{x - 4}$

✒ Simplify.

29) $\sqrt{\dfrac{625}{36}}$

30) $\sqrt{\dfrac{1296}{25}}$

31) $\sqrt{\dfrac{147}{64}}$

32) $\sqrt{\dfrac{98}{18}}$

Chapter 13: Answers

1) 7

2) 18

3) $8x$

4) 17

5) $5b^2$

6) $3x$

7) $7\sqrt{6}$

8) $12\sqrt{2}$

9) $-6\sqrt{7}$

10) $19\sqrt{2}$

11) $-4\sqrt{3}$

12) $4\sqrt{x}$

13) 12

14) $30y$

15) -72

16) $27b\sqrt{2}$

17) $-\dfrac{(1+\sqrt{5})(1+\sqrt{3})}{2}$

18) $-\dfrac{2\sqrt{2}+2\sqrt{5}+2\sqrt{3}+\sqrt{30}}{3}$

19) $\dfrac{\sqrt{7}(\sqrt{6}+\sqrt{3})}{3}$

20) $\dfrac{2\sqrt{2}}{a^2}$

21) $x = 10$

22) $x = 20.5$

23) $x = 25$

24) $x = \dfrac{3}{4}$

25) $x \geq -1, y \geq 0$

26) $x \geq 2, y \geq 6$

27) $x \geq 0, y \geq -1$

28) $x \geq 4, y \geq 0$

29) $\dfrac{25}{6}$

30) $\dfrac{36}{5}$

31) $\dfrac{7\sqrt{3}}{8}$

32) $\dfrac{7}{3}$

CHAPTER

14 Geometry and Solid Figures

Math topics that you'll learn in this chapter:

- ☑ The Pythagorean Theorem
- ☑ Complementary and Supplementary angles
- ☑ Parallel lines and Transversals
- ☑ Triangles
- ☑ Special Right Triangles
- ☑ Polygons
- ☑ Circles
- ☑ Trapezoids
- ☑ Cubes
- ☑ Rectangle Prisms
- ☑ Cylinder

173

The Pythagorean Theorem

- You can use the Pythagorean Theorem to find a missing side in a right triangle.

- In any right triangle: $a^2 + b^2 = c^2$

Examples:

Example 1. Right triangle ABC (not shown) has two legs of lengths 3 cm (AB) and 4 cm (AC). What is the length of the hypotenuse of the triangle (side BC)?

Solution: Use Pythagorean Theorem: $a^2 + b^2 = c^2$, $a = 3$, and $b = 4$

Then: $a^2 + b^2 = c^2 \rightarrow 3^2 + 4^2 = c^2 \rightarrow 9 + 16 = c^2 \rightarrow 25 = c^2 \rightarrow c = \sqrt{25} = 5$

The length of the hypotenuse is 5 cm.

Example 2. Find the hypotenuse of this triangle.

Solution: Use Pythagorean Theorem: $a^2 + b^2 = c^2$

Then: $a^2 + b^2 = c^2 \rightarrow 8^2 + 6^2 = c^2 \rightarrow 64 + 36 = c^2$

$c^2 = 100 \rightarrow c = \sqrt{100} = 10$

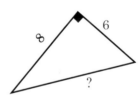

Example 3. Find the length of the missing side in this triangle.

Solution: Use Pythagorean Theorem: $a^2 + b^2 = c^2$

Then: $a^2 + b^2 = c^2 \rightarrow 12^2 + b^2 = 15^2 \rightarrow 144 + b^2 = 225 \rightarrow$

$b^2 = 225 - 144 \rightarrow b^2 = 81 \rightarrow b = \sqrt{81} = 9$

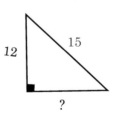

Complementary and Supplementary angles

- Two angles with a sum of 90 degrees are called complementary angles.

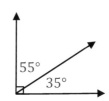

- Two angles with a sum of 180 degrees are Supplementary angles.

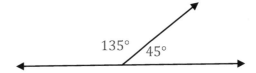

Examples:

Example 1. Find the missing angle.

Solution: Notice that the two angles form a right angle. This means that the angles are complementary, and their sum is 90. Then: $18 + x = 90 \rightarrow x = 90° - 18° = 72°$
The missing angle is 72 degrees. $x = 72°$

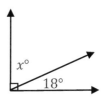

Example 2. Angles Q and S are supplementary. What is the measure of angle Q if angle S is 35 degrees?

Solution: Q and S are supplementary $\rightarrow Q + S = 180 \rightarrow Q + 35 = 180 \rightarrow$
$$Q = 180 - 35 = 145$$

Example 3. Angles x and y are complementary. What is the measure of angle x if angle y is 16 degrees?

Solution: Angles x and y are complementary $\rightarrow x + y = 90 \rightarrow x + 16 = 90 \rightarrow$
$$x = 90 - 16 = 74$$

bit.ly/3nlOn6G

Find more at

Parallel lines and Transversals

- When a line (transversal) intersects two parallel lines in the same plane, eight angles are formed. In the following diagram, a transversal intersects two parallel lines. Angles 1, 3, 5, and 7 are congruent. Angles 2, 4, 6, and 8 are also congruent.

- In the following diagram, the following angles are supplementary angles (their sum is 180):

  ❖ Angles 1 and 8

  ❖ Angles 2 and 7

  ❖ Angles 3 and 6

  ❖ Angles 4 and 5

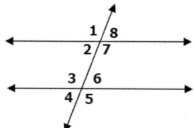

Example:

In the following diagram, two parallel lines are cut by a transversal. What is the value of x?

Solution: The two angles $3x - 15$ and $2x + 7$ are equivalent.

That is: $3x - 15 = 2x + 7$

Now, solve for x:

$3x - 15 + 15 = 2x + 7 + 15$

$\rightarrow 3x = 2x + 22 \rightarrow 3x - 2x = 2x + 22 - 2x \rightarrow$

$x = 22$

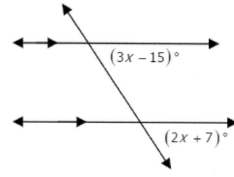

Triangles

- In any triangle, the sum of all angles is 180 degrees.
- Area of a triangle $= \frac{1}{2} (base \times height)$

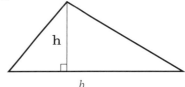

Examples:

Example 1. What is the area of this triangles?

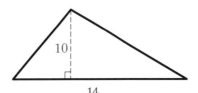

Solution: Use the area formula:

Area $= \frac{1}{2} (base \times height)$

$base = 14$ and $height = 10$, Then:

Area $= \frac{1}{2} (14 \times 10) = \frac{1}{2} (140) = 70$

Example 2. What is the area of this triangles?

Solution: Use the area formula:

Area $= \frac{1}{2} (base \times height)$

$base = 16$ and $height = 8$; Area $= \frac{1}{2} (16 \times 8) = \frac{128}{2} = 64$

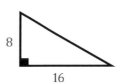

Example 3. What is the missing angle in this triangle?

Solution:

In any triangle, the sum of all angles is 180 degrees.

Let x be the missing angle.

Then: $55 + 80 + x = 180 \rightarrow 135 + x = 180 \rightarrow$

$\qquad x = 180 - 135 = 45$

The missing angle is 45 degrees.

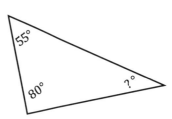

Find more at
bit.ly/3haZrRg

Special Right Triangles

-   A special right triangle is a triangle whose sides are in a particular ratio. Two special right triangles are $45° - 45° - 90°$ and $30° - 60° - 90°$ triangles.

-   In a special $45° - 45° - 90°$ triangle, the three angles are $45°$, $45°$ and $90°$. The lengths of the sides of this triangle are in the ratio of $1:1:\sqrt{2}$.

-   In a special triangle $30° - 60° - 90°$, the three angles are $30° - 60° - 90°$. The lengths of this triangle are in the ratio of $1:\sqrt{3}:2$.

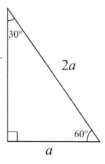

Examples:

Example 1. Find the length of the hypotenuse of a right triangle if the length of the other two sides are both 4 inches.

Solution: this is a right triangle with two equal sides. Therefore, it must be a $45° - 45° - 90°$ triangle. Two equivalent sides are 4 inches. The ratio of sides: $x:x:x\sqrt{2}$

The length of the hypotenuse is $4\sqrt{2}$ inches. $x:x:x\sqrt{2} \rightarrow 4:4:4\sqrt{2}$

Example 2. The length of the hypotenuse of a right triangle is 6 inches. What are the lengths of the other two sides if one angle of the triangle is $30°$?

Solution: The hypotenuse is 6 inches and the triangle is a $30° - 60° - 90°$ triangle. Then, one side of the triangle is 3 (it's half the side of the hypotenuse) and the other side is $3\sqrt{3}$. (it's the smallest side times $\sqrt{3}$)

$x:x\sqrt{3}:2x \rightarrow x = 3 \rightarrow x:x\sqrt{3}:2x = 3:3\sqrt{3}:6$

Polygons

- The perimeter of a square $= 4 \times side = 4s$

- The perimeter of a rectangle $= 2(width + length)$

- The perimeter of trapezoid $= a + b + c + d$

- The perimeter of a regular hexagon $= 6a$

- The perimeter of a parallelogram $= 2(l + w)$

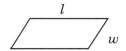

Examples:

Example 1. Find the perimeter of following regular hexagon.

Solution: Since the hexagon is regular, all sides are equal.
Then, the perimeter of the hexagon $= 6 \times (one\ side)$
The perimeter of the hexagon $= 6 \times (one\ side) = 6 \times 8 = 48\ m$

Example 2. Find the perimeter of following trapezoid.

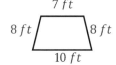

Solution: The perimeter of a trapezoid $= a + b + c + d$
The perimeter of the trapezoid $= 7 + 8 + 8 + 10 = 33\ ft$

Circles

- In a circle, variable r is usually used for the radius and d for diameter.

- *Area of a circle* $= \pi r^2$ (π is about 3.14)

- *Circumference of a circle* $= 2\pi r$

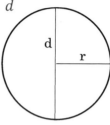

Examples:

Example 1. Find the area of this circle. ($\pi = 3.14$)

Solution:
Use area formula: $Area = \pi r^2$
$r = 6\ in \rightarrow Area = \pi(6)^2 = 36\pi$, $\pi = 3.14$
Then: $Area = 36 \times 3.14 = 113.04\ in^2$

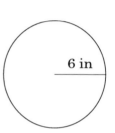

Example 2. Find the Circumference of this circle. ($\pi = 3.14$)

Solution:
Use Circumference formula: $Circumference = 2\pi r$
$r = 8\ cm \rightarrow Circumference = 2\pi(8) = 16\pi$
$\pi = 3.14$, Then: $Circumference = 16 \times 3.14 = 50.24\ cm$

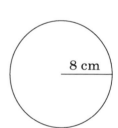

Example 3. Find the area of this circle.

Solution:
Use area formula: $Area = \pi r^2$
$r = 9\ in$, Then: $Area = \pi(9)^2 = 81\pi$, $\pi = 3.14$
$\qquad\qquad Area = 81 \times 3.14 = 254.34\ in^2$

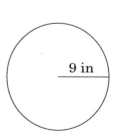

Trapezoids

- A quadrilateral with at least one pair of parallel sides is a trapezoid.

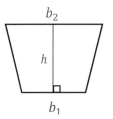

- Area of a trapezoid $= \frac{1}{2}h(b_1 + b_2)$

Examples:

Example 1. Calculate the area of this trapezoid.

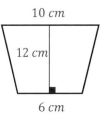

Solution:

Use area formula: $A = \frac{1}{2}h(b_1 + b_2)$

$b_1 = 6\ cm$, $b_2 = 10\ cm$ and $h = 12\ cm$

Then: $A = \frac{1}{2}(12)(10 + 6) = 6(16) = 96\ cm^2$

Example 2. Calculate the area of this trapezoid.

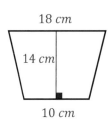

Solution:

Use area formula: $A = \frac{1}{2}h(b_1 + b_2)$

$b_1 = 10\ cm$, $b_2 = 18\ cm$ and $h = 14\ cm$

Then: $A = \frac{1}{2}(14)(10 + 18) = 196\ cm^2$

bit.ly/3hpKACJ

Find more at

Cubes

- A cube is a three-dimensional solid object bounded by six square sides.

- Volume is the measure of the amount of space inside of a solid figure, like a cube, ball, cylinder or pyramid.

- The volume of a cube = $(one\ side)^3$

- The surface area of a cube = $6 \times (one\ side)^2$

Examples:

Example 1. Find the volume and surface area of this cube.

Solution: Use volume formula: $volume = (one\ side)^3$
Then: $volume = (one\ side)^3 = (3)^3 = 27\ cm^3$
Use surface area formula:
$surface\ area\ of\ a\ cube$: $6(one\ side)^2 = 6(3)^2 = 6(9) = 54\ cm^2$

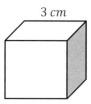
3 cm

Example 2. Find the volume and surface area of this cube.

Solution: Use volume formula: $volume = (one\ side)^3$
Then: $volume = (one\ side)^3 = (6)^3 = 216\ cm^3$
Use surface area formula:
$surface\ area\ of\ a\ cube$: $6(one\ side)^2 = 6(6)^2 = 6(36) = 216\ cm^2$

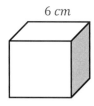
6 cm

Example 3. Find the volume and surface area of this cube.

Solution: Use volume formula: $volume = (one\ side)^3$
Then: $volume = (one\ side)^3 = (8)^3 = 512\ m^3$
Use surface area formula:
$surface\ area\ of\ a\ cube$: $6(one\ side)^2 = 6(8)^2 = 6(64) = 384\ m^2$

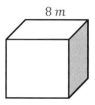
8 m

Rectangular Prisms

- A rectangular prism is a solid 3-dimensional object with six rectangular faces.

- The volume of a rectangular prism = *Length × Width × Height*

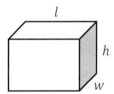

$Volume = l \times w \times h$

$Surface\ area = 2 \times (wh + lw + lh)$

Examples:

Example 1. Find the volume and surface area of this rectangular prism.

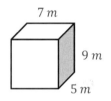

Solution: Use volume formula: $Volume = l \times w \times h$

Then: $Volume = 7 \times 5 \times 9 = 315\ m^3$

Use surface area formula: $Surface\ area = 2 \times (wh + lw + lh)$

Then: $Surface\ area = 2 \times \big((5 \times 9) + (7 \times 5) + (7 \times 9)\big)$

$= 2 \times (45 + 35 + 63) = 2 \times (143) = 286\ m^2$

Example 2. Find the volume and surface area of this rectangular prism.

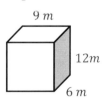

Solution: Use volume formula: $Volume = l \times w \times h$

Then: $Volume = 9 \times 6 \times 12 = 648\ m^3$

Use surface area formula: $Surface\ area = 2 \times (wh + lw + lh)$

Then: $Surface\ area = 2 \times \big((6 \times 12) + (9 \times 6) + (9 \times 12)\big)$

$= 2 \times (72 + 54 + 108) = 2 \times (234) = 468\ m^2$

bit.ly/3nKm2GT

Find more at

Cylinder

- A cylinder is a solid geometric figure with straight parallel sides and a circular or oval cross-section.

- *Volume of a Cylinder = π(radius)² × height, π ≈ 3.14*

- *Surface area of a cylinder = 2πr² + 2πrh*

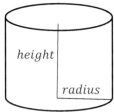

Examples:

Example 1. Find the volume and Surface area of the follow Cylinder.

Solution: Use volume formula:

Volume = π(radius)² × height

Then: *Volume = π(4)² × 10 = 16π × 10 = 160π*

π = 3.14, then: *Volume = 160π = 160 × 3.14 = 502.4 cm³*

Use surface area formula: *Surface area = 2πr² + 2πrh*

Then: 2π(4)² + 2π(4)(10) = 2π(16) + 2π(40) = 32π + 80π = 112π

π = 3.14 , Then: *Surface area = 112 × 3.14 = 351.68 cm²*

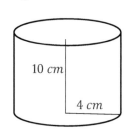

Example 2. Find the volume and Surface area of the follow Cylinder.

Solution: Use volume formula:

Volume = π(radius)² × height

Then: *Volume = π(5)² × 8 = 25 π × 8 = 200π*

π = 3.14, Then: *Volume = 200π = 628 cm³*

Use surface area formula: *Surface area = 2πr² + 2πrh*

Then: = 2π(5)² + 2π(5)(8) = 2π(25) + 2π(40) = 50π + 80π = 130π

π = 3.14 then: *Surface area = 130 × 3.14 = 408.2 cm²*

bit.ly/37LtcVM

Find more at

Chapter 14: Practices

✒ Find the missing side?

1)
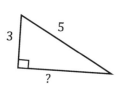

2)
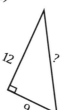

3)
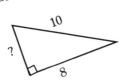

4)
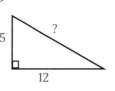

✒ Find the measure of the unknown angle in each triangle.

5)
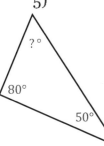

6)
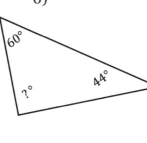

7)
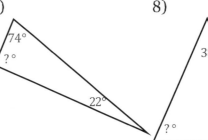

8)

✒ Find the area of each triangle.

9)
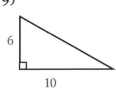

10)
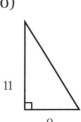

11)
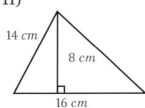

12)
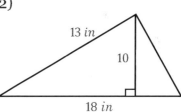

✒ Find the perimeter or circumference of each shape.

13)
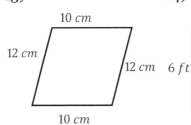

14)
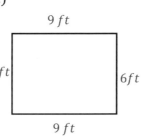

15)
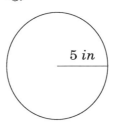

16) *regular hexagon*
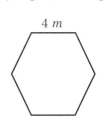

✎ **Find the area of each trapezoid.**

17)   18)   19)   20)

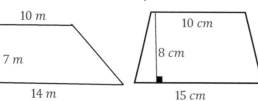
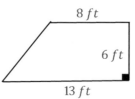
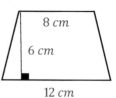

✎ **Find the volume of each cube.**

21)   22)   23)   24)

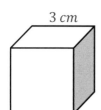
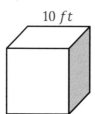
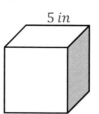
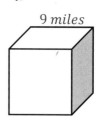

✎ **Find the volume of each Rectangular Prism.**

25)   26)   27)

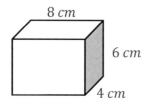
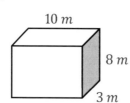
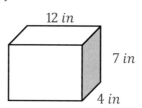

✎ **Find the volume of each Cylinder. Round your answer to the nearest tenth. ($\pi = 3.14$)**

28)   29)   30)

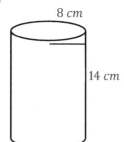
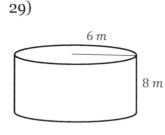
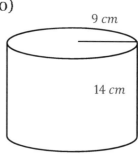

Chapter 14: Answers

1) 4

2) 15

3) 6

4) 13

5) 50

6) 76

7) 84

8) 70

9) 30

10) 49.5

11) $64\ cm^2$

12) $90\ in^2$

13) $44\ cm$

14) $30\ ft$

15) $10\ \pi \approx 31.4\ in$

16) $24\ m$

17) $84\ m^2$

18) $100\ cm^2$

19) $63\ ft^2$

20) $60\ cm^2$

21) $27\ cm^3$

22) $1,000\ ft^3$

23) $125\ in^3$

24) $729\ mi^3$

25) $192\ cm^3$

26) $240\ m^3$

27) $336\ in^3$

28) $2,813.44\ cm^3$

29) $904.32\ m^3$

30) $3,560.76\ cm^3$

CHAPTER

15 Statistics

Math topics that you'll learn in this chapter:

- ☑ Mean, Median, Mode, and Range of the Given Data
- ☑ Pie Graph
- ☑ Probability Problems
- ☑ Permutations and Combinations

189

Mean, Median, Mode, and Range of the Given Data

- **Mean:** $\dfrac{sum\ of\ the\ data}{total\ number\ of\ data\ entires}$

- **Mode:** the value in the list that appears most often

- **Median:** is the middle number of a group of numbers arranged in order by size.

- **Range:** the difference of the largest value and smallest value in the list

Examples:

Example 1. What is the mode of these numbers? $5, 6, 8, 6, 8, 5, 3, 5$

Solution: Mode: the value in the list that appears most often.
Therefore, the mode is number 5. There are three number 5 in the data.

Example 2. What is the median of these numbers? $6, 11, 15, 10, 17, 20, 7$

Solution: Write the numbers in order: $6, 7, 10, 11, 15, 17, 20$
The median is the number in the middle. Therefore, the median is 11.

Example 3. What is the mean of these numbers? $7, 2, 3, 2, 4, 8, 7, 5$

Solution: Mean: $\dfrac{sum\ of\ the\ data}{total\ number\ of\ data\ entires} = \dfrac{7+2+3+2+4+8+7+5}{8} = \dfrac{38}{8} = 4.75$

Example 4. What is the range in this list? $3, 7, 12, 6, 15, 20, 8$

Solution: Range is the difference of the largest value and smallest value in the list. The largest value is 20 and the smallest value is 3.
Then: $20 - 3 = 17$

Pie Graph

- A Pie Graph (Pie Chart) is a circle chart divided into sectors, each sector represents the relative size of each value.

- Pie charts represent a snapshot of how a group is broken down into smaller pieces.

Examples:

A library has 750 books that include Mathematics, Physics, Chemistry, English and History. Use the following graph to answer the questions.

Example 1. What is the number of Mathematics books?

Solution: Number of total books = 750
Percent of Mathematics books = 28%
Then, the number of Mathematics books: 28% × 750 = 0.28 × 750 = 210

Example 2. What is the number of History books?

Solution: Number of total books = 750
Percent of History books = 12%
Then: 0.12 × 750 = 90

Example 3. What is the number of Chemistry books in the library?

Solution: Number of total books = 750
Percent of Chemistry books = 22%
Then: 0.22 × 750 = 165

Probability Problems

- Probability is the likelihood of something happening in the future. It is expressed as a number between zero (can never happen) to 1 (will always happen).

- Probability can be expressed as a fraction, a decimal, or a percent.

- Probability formula: $Probability = \frac{number\ of\ desired\ outcomes}{number\ of\ total\ outcomes}$

Examples:

Example 1. Anita's trick–or–treat bag contains 10 pieces of chocolate, 16 suckers, 16 pieces of gum, 22 pieces of licorice. If she randomly pulls a piece of candy from her bag, what is the probability of her pulling out a piece of sucker?

Solution: Probability $= \frac{number\ of\ desired\ outcomes}{number\ of\ total\ outcomes}$

Probability of pulling out a piece of sucker $= \frac{16}{10 + 16 + 16 + 22} = \frac{16}{64} = \frac{1}{4}$

Example 2. A bag contains 20 balls: four green, five black, eight blue, a brown, a red and one white. If 19 balls are removed from the bag at random, what is the probability that a brown ball has been removed?

Solution: If 19 balls are removed from the bag at random, there will be one ball in the bag. The probability of choosing a brown ball is 1 out of 20. Therefore, the probability of not choosing a brown ball is 19 out of 20 and the probability of having not a brown ball after removing 19 balls is the same. The answer is: $\frac{19}{20}$

Permutations and Combinations

Factorials are products, indicated by an exclamation mark. For example, $4! = 4 \times 3 \times 2 \times 1$ (Remember that $0!$ is defined to be equal to 1)

- **Permutations:** The number of ways to choose a sample of k elements from a set of n distinct objects where order does matter, and replacements are not allowed. For a permutation problem, use this formula:

$$_n\mathrm{P}_k = \frac{n!}{(n-k)!}$$

- **Combination:** The number of ways to choose a sample of r elements from a set of n distinct objects where order does not matter, and replacements are not allowed. For a combination problem, use this formula:

$$_n\mathrm{C}_r = \frac{n!}{r!\,(n-r)!}$$

Examples:

Example 1. How many ways can the first and second place be awarded to 7 people?

Solution: Since the order matters, (the first and second place are different!) we need to use permutation formula where n is 7 and k is 2. Then: $\frac{n!}{(n-k)!} = \frac{7!}{(7-2)!} = \frac{7!}{5!} = \frac{7 \times 6 \times 5!}{5!}$, remove $5!$ from both sides of the fraction. Then: $\frac{7 \times 6 \times 5!}{5!} = 7 \times 6 = 42$

Example 2. How many ways can we pick a team of 3 people from a group of 8?

Solution: Since the order doesn't matter, we need to use a combination formula where n is 8 and r is 3.
Then: $\frac{n!}{r!\,(n-r)!} = \frac{8!}{3!\,(8-3)!} = \frac{8!}{3!\,(5)!} = \frac{8 \times 7 \times 6 \times 5!}{3!\,(5)!} = \frac{8 \times 7 \times 6}{3 \times 2 \times 1} = \frac{336}{6} = 56$

Chapter 15: Practices

✍ Find the values of the Given Data.

1) 6, 11, 5, 3, 6

   Mode: _____   Range: _____

   Mean: _____   Median: _____

2) 4, 9, 1, 9, 6, 7

   Mode: _____   Range: _____

   Mean: _____   Median: _____

3) 10, 3, 6, 10, 4, 15

   Mode: _____   Range: _____

   Mean: _____   Median: _____

4) 12, 4, 8, 9, 3, 12, 15

   Mode: _____   Range: _____

   Mean: _____   Median: _____

✍ The circle graph below shows all Bob's expenses for last month. Bob spent $790 on his Rent last month.

5) How much did Bob's total expenses last month? _____

6) How much did Bob spend for foods last month? _____

7) How much did Bob spend for his bills last month? _____

8) How much did Bob spend on his car last month? _____

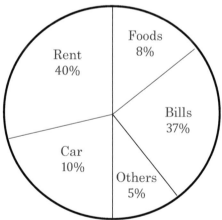

Bob's last month expenses

Rent 40%
Foods 8%
Bills 37%
Car 10%
Others 5%

✎ **Solve.**

9) Bag A contains 8 red marbles and 6 green marbles. Bag B contains 5 black marbles and 7 orange marbles. What is the probability of selecting a green marble at random from bag A? What is the probability of selecting a black marble at random from Bag B?

_____   _____

✎ **Solve.**

10) Susan is baking cookies. She uses sugar, flour, butter, and eggs. How many different orders of ingredients can she try? _____

11) Jason is planning for his vacation. He wants to go to museum, go to the beach, and play volleyball. How many different ways of ordering are there for him? _____

12) In how many ways can a team of 6 basketball players choose a captain and co-captain? _____

13) How many ways can you give 5 balls to your 8 friends? _____

14) A professor is going to arrange her 5 students in a straight line. In how many ways can she do this? _____

15) In how many ways can a teacher chooses 12 out of 15 students? _____

bit.ly/3RAbyde
Solutions at

Chapter 15: Answers

1) Mode: 6, Range: 8, Mean: 6.2, Median: 6

2) Mode: 9, Range:8, Mean: 6, Median: 6.5

3) Mode: 10, Range: 12, Mean: 8, Median: 8

4) Mode: 12, Range: 12, Mean: 9, Median: 9

5) $1,975

6) $158

7) $730.75

8) $197.50

9) $\frac{3}{7}, \frac{5}{12}$

10) 24

11) 6

12) 30 (it's a permutation problem)

13) 56 (it's a combination problem)

14) 120

15) 455 (it's a combination problem)

Time to test

Time to refine your math skill with a practice test

In this section, there are two complete TSI Mathematics Tests. Take a practice TSI Math test to simulate the test day experience. After you've finished, score your test using the answer keys.

Before You Start

- You'll need a pencil and a calculator to take the test.
- For each question, there are four possible answers. Choose which one is best.
- It's okay to guess. There is no penalty for wrong answers.
- After you've finished the test, review the answer key to see where you went wrong.

Good Luck!

TSI Mathematics Practice Test 1

2023

20 questions

Total time for this section: No time limit.

You may use a calculator on this test.

(On a real TSI test, there is an onscreen calculator to use on most questions.)

1) What is 5 percent of 480?

A. 20

B. 24

C. 30

D. 40

2) Last week 24,000 fans attended a football match. This week three times as many bought tickets, but one sixth of them cancelled their tickets. How many are attending this week?

A. 48,000

B. 54,000

C. 60,000

D. 72,000

3) Bob deposits 15% of $160 into a savings account, what is the amount of his deposit?

A. $10

B. $16

C. $20

D. $24

4) A bank is offering 3.5% simple interest on a savings account. If you deposit $12,000, how much interest will you earn in two years?

A. $420

B. $840

C. $4200

D. $8,400

5) If a gas tank can hold 28 gallons, how many gallons does it contain when it is $\frac{3}{4}$ full?

A. 84

B. 168

C. 33.5

D. 21

6) Ethan needs an 75% average in his writing class to pass. On his first 4 exams, he earned scores of 68%, 72%, 85%, and 90%. What is the minimum score Ethan can earn on his fifth and final test to pass?

A. 80%

B. 70%

C. 68%

D. 60%

$$\frac{5}{8}, 0.625\%, 0.0625$$

7) Which of the following correctly orders the values above from greatest to least?

A. $0.625\%, \frac{5}{8}, 0.0625$

B. $0.0625, 0.625\%, \frac{5}{8}$

C. $\frac{5}{8}, 0.625\%, 0.0625$

D. $\frac{5}{8}, 0.0625, 0.625\%$

8) In a stadium the ratio of home fans to visiting fans in a crowd is $5:7$. Which of the following could be the total number of fans in the stadium?

A. 12,324

B. 42,326

C. 44,566

D. 66,812

9) Which of the following points lies on the line $2x - y = -6$?

A. $(-1, 4)$

B. $(2, 2)$

C. $(1, 3)$

D. $(3, 1)$

10) The perimeter of a rectangular yard is 60 meters. What is its length if its width is twice its length?

A. 10 *meters*

B. 18 *meters*

C. 20 *meters*

D. 24 *meters*

11) The mean of 50 test scores was calculated as 88. But, it turned out that one of the scores was misread as 94 but it was 69. What is the correct mean of the test scores?

A. 85

B. 87

C. 87.5

D. 88.5

12) Two dice are thrown simultaneously, what is the probability of getting a sum of 6 or 9?

A. $\frac{1}{3}$

B. $\frac{1}{4}$

C. $\frac{1}{6}$

D. $\frac{1}{12}$

13) A swimming pool holds 2,000 cubic feet of water. The swimming pool is 25 feet long and 10 feet wide. How deep is the swimming pool?

A. 2

B. 4

C. 6

D. 8

14) What is the area of a square whose diagonal is 8?

A. 16

B. 32

C. 36

D. 64

15) The average of 6 numbers is 12. The average of 4 of those numbers is 10. What is the average of the other two numbers?

A. 10

B. 12

C. 14

D. 16

16) The perimeter of the trapezoid below (not drawn to scale) is 38 *cm*. What is its area?

13 *cm*

A. 576 cm^2

B. 78 cm^2

C. 48 cm^2

D. 24 cm^2

4 *cm*

9 *cm*

17) What is the value of x in the following equation?

$$\frac{2}{3}x + \frac{1}{6} = \frac{1}{3}$$

A. 6

B. $\frac{1}{2}$

C. $\frac{1}{3}$

D. $\frac{1}{4}$

18) Right triangle *ABC* has two legs of lengths 5 *cm* (*AB*) and 12 *cm* (*AC*). What is the length of the third side (*BC*)?

A. 4 *cm*

B. 6 *cm*

C. 8 *cm*

D. 13 *cm*

19) What is the equivalent temperature of $104°F$ in Celsius?

$$C = \frac{5}{9}(F - 32)$$

A. 32

B. 40

C. 48

D. 52

20) Find the solution (x, y) to the following system of equations?

$$2x + 5y = 11$$
$$4x - 2y = -14$$

A. $(14, 5)$

B. $(6, 8)$

C. $(11, 17)$

D. $(-2, 3)$

STOP: This is the End of Test 1.

TSI Mathematics
Practice Test 2

2023

20 questions

Total time for this section: No time limit.

You may NOT use a calculator on this Section.

(On a real TSI test, there is an onscreen calculator to use on some questions.)

1) 12% of what number is equal to 72?

A. 11.25

B. 112.50

C. 400

D. 600

2) The price of a sofa is decreased by 20% to $476. What was its original price?

A. $480

B. $520

C. $595

D. $600

3) Which of the following expressions has the same value as $\frac{5}{4} \times \frac{6}{2}$?

A. $\frac{6 \times 3}{4}$

B. $\frac{6 \times 2}{4}$

C. $\frac{5 \times 6}{4}$

D. $\frac{5 \times 3}{4}$

4) $\frac{(8+6)^2}{2} + 6 = ?$

A. 110

B. 104

C. 90

D. 14

5) A rope weighs 600 grams per meter of length. What is the weight in kilograms of 14.2 meters of this rope? ($1 \, kilograms = 1000 \, grams$)

A. 0.0852

B. 0.852

C. 8.52

D. 85.20

6) When a number is subtracted from 28 and the difference is divided by that number, the result is 3. What is the value of the number?

A. 2

B. 4

C. 7

D. 12

7) An angle is equal to one fifth of its supplement. What is the measure of that angle?

A. 30

B. 34

C. 36

D. 45

8) John traveled 150 km in 5 hours and Alice traveled 180 km in 4 hours. What is the ratio of the average speed of John to average speed of Alice?

A. 3: 2

B. 2: 5

C. 2: 3

D. 5: 6

9) Right triangle ABC has two legs of lengths 6 cm (AB) and 8 cm (AC). What is the length of the third side (BC)?

A. 6 cm

B. 8 cm

C. 10 cm

D. 14 cm

10) The area of a circle is less than 49π. Which of the following can be the circumference of the circle?

A. 12π

B. 14π

C. 24π

D. 32π

11) The width of a box is one third of its length. The height of the box is one third of its width. If the length of the box is 36 cm, what is the volume of the box?

A. 81 cm^3

B. 162 cm^3

C. C.243 cm^3

D. 1,728 cm^3

12) In the xy-plane, the point $(4,3)$ and $(3,2)$ are on line A. Which of the following points could also be on line A?

A. $(-1, 2)$

B. $(5, 7)$

C. $(3, 4)$

D. $(-1, -2)$

13) A construction company is building a wall. The company can build 40 cm of the wall per minute. After 50 minutes construction, $\frac{2}{3}$ of the wall is completed. How high is the wall?

A. 10 m

B. 15 m

C. 30 m

D. 35 m

14) The average of five consecutive numbers is 40. What is the smallest number?

A. 40

B. 38

C. 34

D. 12

15) The average weight of 18 girls in a class is 55 kg and the average weight of 32 boys in the same class is 62 kg. What is the average weight of all the 50 students in that class?

A. 58

B. 59.48

C. 61.68

D. 62.90

16) The surface area of a cylinder is $150\pi \ cm^2$. If its height is $10 \ cm$, what is the radius of the cylinder?

A. $13 \ cm$

B. $11 \ cm$

C. $15 \ cm$

D. $5 \ cm$

17) If $x + y = 0$, $4x - 2y = 24$, which of the following ordered pairs (x, y) satisfies both equations?

A. $(4, 3)$

B. $(5, 4)$

C. $(4, -4)$

D. $(4, -6)$

18) If $f(x) = 3x + 4(x + 1) + 2$ then $f(3x) =?$

A. $21x + 6$

B. $16x - 6$

C. $25x + 4$

D. $12x + 3$

19) A line in the xy-plane passes through origin and has a slope of $\frac{1}{3}$. Which of the following points lies on the line?

A. $(2,1)$

B. $(4,1)$

C. $(9,3)$

D. $(6,3)$

20) Which of the following is equivalent to $(3n^2 + 4n + 6) - (2n^2 - 5)$?

A. $n + 4n^2$

B. $n^2 - 3$

C. $n^2 + 4n + 11$

D. $n + 2$

STOP: This is the End of Test 2.

TSI Mathematics Practice Test Answers Key

Now, it's time to review your results to see where you went wrong and what areas you need to improve!

TSI Mathematics Practice Test 1				TSI Mathematics Practice Test 2			
1	B	11	C	1	D	11	D
2	C	12	B	2	C	12	D
3	D	13	D	3	D	13	C
4	B	14	B	4	B	14	B
5	D	15	D	5	C	15	B
6	D	16	B	6	C	16	D
7	D	17	D	7	A	17	C
8	A	18	D	8	C	18	A
9	A	19	B	9	C	19	C
10	A	20	D	10	A	20	C

TSI Mathematics Practice Test
Answers and Explanations

TSI Mathematics Practice Test 1

1) Choice B is correct.

5 percent of $480 = \frac{5}{100} \times 480 = \frac{1}{20} \times 480 = \frac{480}{20} = 24$

2) Choice C is correct

Three times of 24,000 is 72,000. One sixth of them cancelled their tickets.

One sixth of 72,000 equals 12,000 ($\frac{1}{6} \times 72{,}000 = 12{,}000$).

60,000(72,000 − 12,000 = 60,000) fans are attending this week

3) Choice D is correct

15% of $160 is $0.15 \times 160 = 24$

4) Choice B is correct

Use simple interest formula: $I = prt$ (I = interest, p = principal, r = rate, t = time)

$I = (12{,}000)(0.035)(2) = 840$

5) Choice D is correct

$\frac{3}{4} \times 28 = \frac{84}{4} = 21$

6) Choice D is correct

Ethan needs an 75% average to pass for five exams. Therefore, the sum of 5 exams must be at lease $5 \times 75 = 375$, The sum of 4 exams is: $68 + 72 + 85 + 90 = 315$.

The minimum score Jason can earn on his fifth and final test to pass is: $375 - 315 = 60$

7) Choice D is correct

To best compare the numbers, they should be put in the same format. The percent 0.625% can be converted to a decimal by dividing 0.625 by 100, which gives 0.00625. $\frac{5}{8}$ can be converted to a decimal by dividing 5 by 8, which gives 0.625. Now, all three numbers are in decimal format. $0.625 > 0.0625 > 0.00625$ or $\frac{5}{8} > 0.0625 > 0.625\%$, which is choice D.

8) Choice A is correct

In the stadium the ratio of home fans to visiting fans in a crowd is $5 : 7$. Therefore, total number of fans must be divisible by 12: $5 + 7 = 12$. Let's review the choices:

A. $12,324$: $12,324 \div 12 = 1,027$

B. $42,326$ $42,326 \div 12 = 3,527.166$

C. $44,566$ $44,566 \div 12 = 3,713.833$

D. $66,812$ $66,812 \div 12 = 5,567.666$

Only choice A when divided by 12 results a whole number.

9) Choice A is correct

$2x - y = -6$. Plug in the values of x and y from choices provided. Then:

A. $(-1, 4)$ $2x - y = -6 \rightarrow 2(-1) - 4 = -6 \rightarrow -2 - 4 = -6$ This is true!

B. $(2, 2)$ $2x - y = -6 \rightarrow 2(2) - 2 = -6 \rightarrow 4 - 2 = -6$ This is NOT true!

C. $(1, 3)$ $2x - y = -6 \rightarrow 2(1) - 3 = -6 \rightarrow 2 - 3 = -6$ This is NOT true!

D. $(3, 1)$ $2x - y = -6 \rightarrow 2(3) - 1 = -6 \rightarrow 6 - 1 = -6$ This is NOT true!

10) Choice A is correct

The width of the rectangle is twice its length. Let x be the length. Then, $width = 2x$

Perimeter of the rectangle is $2 \ (width + length) = 2(2x + x) = 60 \Rightarrow 6x = 60 \Rightarrow x = 10$

Length of the rectangle is 10 meters.

11) Choice C is correct

$average \ (mean) = \dfrac{sum \ of \ terms}{number \ of \ terms} \Rightarrow 88 = \dfrac{sum \ of \ terms}{50} \Rightarrow sum = 88 \times 50 = 4,400$

The difference of 94 and 69 is 25. Therefore, 25 should be subtracted from the sum.

$4,400 - 25 = 4,375, \ mean = \dfrac{sum \ of \ terms}{number \ of \ terms} \Rightarrow mean = \dfrac{4,375}{50} = 87.5$

12) Choice B is correct

To get a sum of 6 for two dice, we can get 5 different options:

$(5, 1), (4, 2), (3, 3), (2, 4), (1, 5)$, To get a sum of 9 for two dice, we can get 4 different options: $(6, 3), (5, 4), (4, 5), (3, 6)$, Therefore, there are 9 options to get the sum of 6 or 9.

Since, we have $6 \times 6 = 36$ total options, the probability of getting a sum of 6 and 9 is 9 out of 36 or $\dfrac{1}{4}$.

13) Choice D is correct

Use formula of rectangle prism volume.

$V = (length)(width)(height) \Rightarrow 2,000 = (25)(10)(height) \Rightarrow height = 2,000 \div 250 = 8$

14) Choice B is correct

The diagonal of the square is 8. Let x be the side.

Use Pythagorean Theorem: $a^2 + b^2 = c^2$

$x^2 + x^2 = 8^2 \Rightarrow 2x^2 = 8^2 \Rightarrow 2x^2 = 64 \Rightarrow x^2 = 32 \Rightarrow x = \sqrt{32}$

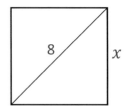

The area of the square is: $\sqrt{32} \times \sqrt{32} = 32$

15) Choice D is correct

$average = \frac{sum\ of\ terms}{number\ of\ terms} \Rightarrow$ (average of 6 numbers) $12 = \frac{sum\ of\ numbers}{6} \Rightarrow$ sum of 6 numbers is: $12 \times 6 = 72$

(average of 4 numbers) $10 = \frac{sum\ of\ numbers}{4} \Rightarrow$ sum of 4 numbers is $10 \times 4 = 40$

$sum\ of\ 6\ numbers - sum\ of\ 4\ numbers = sum\ of\ 2\ numbers$: $72 - 40 = 32$

average of 2 numbers $= \frac{32}{2} = 16$

16) Choice B is correct

The perimeter of the trapezoid is 38 cm. Therefore, the missing side is:

$38 - 13 - 9 - 4 = 12$. Area of a trapezoid: $A = \frac{1}{2}h(b_1 + b_2) = \frac{1}{2}(12)(4 + 9) = 78$

17) Choice D is correct

Isolate and solve for x: $\frac{2}{3}x + \frac{1}{6} = \frac{1}{3} \Rightarrow \frac{2}{3}x = \frac{1}{3} - \frac{1}{6} = \frac{1}{6} \Rightarrow \frac{2}{3}x = \frac{1}{6}$

Multiply both sides by the reciprocal of the coefficient of x.

$(\frac{3}{2})\frac{2}{3}x = \frac{1}{6}(\frac{3}{2}) \Rightarrow x = \frac{3}{12} = \frac{1}{4}$

18) Choice D is correct

Use Pythagorean Theorem: $a^2 + b^2 = c^2 \to 5^2 + 12^2 = c^2 \Rightarrow 169 = c^2 \Rightarrow c = 13$

19) Choice B is correct

Plug in 104 for F and then solve for C.

$$C = \frac{5}{9}(F - 32) \Rightarrow C = \frac{5}{9}(104 - 32) \Rightarrow C = \frac{5}{9}(72) = 40$$

20) Choice D is correct

Solving Systems of Equations by Elimination: Multiply the first equation by (-2), then add it to the second equation.

$$\begin{array}{l} -2(2x + 5y = 11) \\ \underline{4x - 2y = -14} \end{array} \Rightarrow \begin{array}{l} -4x - 10y = -22 \\ 4x - 2y = -14 \end{array} \Rightarrow -12y = -36 \Rightarrow y = 3$$

Plug in the value of y into one of the equations and solve for x.

$$2x + 5(3) = 11 \Rightarrow 2x + 15 = 11 \Rightarrow 2x = -4 \Rightarrow x = -2$$

TSI Mathematics Practice Test 2

1) Choice D is correct

Dividing 72 by 12%, which is equivalent to 0.12, gives 600. Therefore, 12% of 600 is 72.

2) Choice C is correct

Let x be the original price. If the price of the sofa is decreased by 20% to \$476, then: $80\% \ of \ x = 476 \Rightarrow 0.80x = 476 \Rightarrow x = 476 \div 0.80 = 595$

3) Choice D is correct.

First simplify the multiplication: $\frac{5}{4} \times \frac{6}{2} = \frac{30}{8} = \frac{15}{4}$, Choice D is equal to $\frac{15}{4}$.

$\frac{5 \times 3}{4} = \frac{15}{4}$

4) Choice B is correct

$\frac{(8 + 6)^2}{2} + 6 = \frac{(14)^2}{2} + 6 = \frac{196}{2} + 6 = 98 + 6 = 104$

5) Choice C is correct

The weight of 14.2 meters of this rope is: $14.2 \times 600 \ g = 8,520 \ g$

$1 \ kg = 1,000 \ g$, therefore, $8,520 \ g \div 1000 = 8.52 \ kg$

6) Choice C is correct

Let x be the number. Write the equation and solve for x. $(28 - x) \div x = 3$

Multiply both sides by x. $(28 - x) = 3x$, then add x both sides. $28 = 4x$, now divide both sides by 4. $x = 7$

7) Choice A is correct

The sum of supplement angles is 180. Let x be that angle. Therefore, $x + 5x = 180$

$6x = 180$, divide both sides by 6: $x = 30$

8) Choice C is correct

The average speed of john is: $150 \div 5 = 30 \ km$, The average speed of Alice is: $180 \div 4 = 45 \ km$, Write the ratio and simplify. $30 : 45 = 2 : 3$

9) Choice C is correct

Use Pythagorean Theorem: $a^2 + b^2 = c^2$

$6^2 + 8^2 = c^2 \Rightarrow 36 + 64 = c^2 \Rightarrow 100 = c^2 \Rightarrow c = 10$

10) Choice A is correct

Area of the circle is less than 14π. Use the formula of areas of circles.

$Area = \pi r^2 \Rightarrow 49\,\pi > \pi r^2 \Rightarrow 49 > r^2 \Rightarrow r < 7$

Radius of the circle is less than 7. Let's put 7 for the radius. Now, use the circumference formula: $Circumference = 2\pi r = 2\pi\,(7) = 14\,\pi$

Since the radius of the circle is less than 7. Then, the circumference of the circle must be less than 14π. Only choice A is less than 14π.

11) Choice D is correct

If the length of the box is 36, then the width of the box is one third of it, 12, and the height of the box is 4 (one third of the width). The volume of the box is:

$V = lwh = (36)(12)(4) = 1,728$

12) Choice D is correct

The equation of a line is in the form of $y = mx + b$, where m is the slope of the line and b is the $y - intercept$ of the line. Two points $(4,3)$ and $(3,2)$ are on line A. Therefore, the slope of the line A is: $slope\ of\ line\ A = \frac{y_2 - y_1}{x_2 - x_1} = \frac{2-3}{3-4} = \frac{-1}{-1} = 1$

The slope of line A is 1. Thus, the formula of the line A is: $y = mx + b = x + b$, choose a point and plug in the values of x and y in the equation to solve for b. Let's choose point $(4,3)$. Then: $y = x + b \to 3 = 4 + b \to b = 3 - 4 = -1$. The equation of line A is:

$y = x - 1$

Now, let's review the choices provided:

A. $(-1, 2)$ $y = x - 1 \to 2 = -1 - 1 = -2$ This is not true.

B. $(5, 7)$ $y = x - 1 \to 7 = 5 - 1 = 4$ This is not true.

C. $(3, 4)$ $y = x - 1 \to 4 = 3 - 1 = 2$ This is not true.

D. $(-1, -2)$ $y = x - 1 \to -2 = -1 - 1 = -2$ This is true!

13) Choice C is correct

The rate of construction company $= \frac{40\ cm}{1\ min} = 40\,\frac{cm}{min}$

Height of the wall after $50\ min = \frac{40\ cm}{1\ min} \times 50\ min = 2,000 cm$

Let x be the height of wall, then $\frac{2}{3}x = 2,000\ cm \to x = \frac{3 \times 2,000}{2} \to x = 3,000\ cm = 30m$

14) Choice B is correct

Let x be the smallest number. Then, these are the numbers: $x, x + 1, x + 2, x + 3, x + 4$

$average = \frac{sum\ of\ terms}{number\ of\ terms} \Rightarrow 40 = \frac{x+(x+1)+(x+2)+(x+3)+(x+4)}{5} \Rightarrow 40 = \frac{5x+10}{5} \Rightarrow 200 = 5x + 10 \Rightarrow 190 = 5x \Rightarrow x = 38$

15) Choice B is correct

$average = \frac{sum\ of\ terms}{number\ of\ terms}$, The sum of the weight of all girls is: $18 \times 55 = 990\ kg$

The sum of the weight of all boys is: $32 \times 62 = 1,984\ kg$, The sum of the weight of all students is: $990 + 1,984 = 2,974\ kg$, $average = \frac{2,974}{50} = 59.48$

16) Choice D is correct

Formula for the Surface area of a cylinder is: $SA = 2\pi r^2 + 2\pi rh$

$\rightarrow 150\pi = 2\pi r^2 + 2\pi r(10) \rightarrow r^2 + 10r - 75 = 0$

$(r + 15)(r - 5) = 0 \rightarrow r = 5 \quad or \quad r = -15\ (unacceptable)$

17) Choice C is correct

Method 1: Plugin the values of x and y provided in the options into both equations.

A. $(4, 3)$ $x + y = 0 \rightarrow 4 + 3 \neq 0$

B. $(5, 4)$ $x + y = 0 \rightarrow 5 + 4 \neq 0$

C. $(4, -4)$ $x + y = 0 \rightarrow 4 + (-4) = 0$

D. $(4, -6)$ $x + y = 0 \rightarrow 4 + (-6) \neq 0$

Only option C is correct.

Method 2: Multiplying each side of $x + y = 0$ by 2 gives $2x + 2y = 0$. Then, adding the corresponding side of $2x + 2y = 0$ and $4x - 2y = 24$ gives $6x = 24$. Dividing each side of $6x = 24$ by 6 gives $x = 4$. Finally, substituting 4 for x in $x + y = 0$, or $y = -4$. Therefore, the solution to the given system of equations is $(4, -4)$.

18) Choice A is correct

If $f(x) = 3x + 4(x + 1) + 2$, then find $f(3x)$ by substituting $3x$ for every x in the function. This gives: $f(3x) = 3(3x) + 4(3x + 1) + 2$

It simplifies to: $f(3x) = 3(3x) + 4(3x + 1) + 2 = 9x + 12x + 4 + 2 = 21x + 6$

19) Choice C is correct

First, find the equation of the line. All lines through the origin are of the form $y = mx$, so the equation is $y = \frac{1}{3}x$. Of the given choices, only choice C (9,3), satisfies this equation:

$y = \frac{1}{3}x \rightarrow 3 = \frac{1}{3}(9) = 3$

20) Choice C is correct

$(3n^2 + 4n + 6) - (2n^2 - 5)$. Add like terms together: $3n^2 - 2n^2 = n^2$

$4n$ doesn't have like terms. $6 - (-5) = 11$

Combine these terms into one expression to find the answer: $n^2 + 4n + 11$

… So Much More Online!

Effortless Math Online TSI Math Center offers a complete study program, including the following:

- ✓ Step-by-step instructions on how to prepare for the TSI Math test

- ✓ Numerous TSI Math worksheets to help you measure your math skills

- ✓ Complete list of TSI Math formulas

- ✓ Video lessons for TSI Math topics

- ✓ Full-length TSI Math practice tests

- ✓ And much more…

No Registration Required.

The Best TSI Math Books!

Download eBooks (in PDF format) Instantly!

download at

Download

Most Popular TSI Math Books!

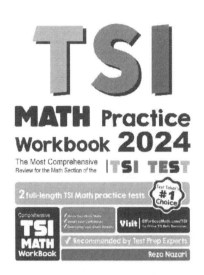

Receive the PDF version of this book or get another FREE book!

Thank you for using our Book!

Do you LOVE this book?

Then, you can get the PDF version of this book or another book absolutely FREE!

Please email us at:

info@EffortlessMath.com

for details.

Author's Final Note

I hope you enjoyed reading this book. You've made it through the book! Great job!

First of all, thank you for purchasing this study guide. I know you could have picked any number of books to help you prepare for your TSI Math test, but you picked this book and for that I am extremely grateful.

It took me years to write this study guide for the TSI Math because I wanted to prepare a comprehensive TSI Math study guide to help test takers make the most effective use of their valuable time while preparing for the test.

After teaching and tutoring math courses for over a decade, I've gathered my personal notes and lessons to develop this study guide. It is my greatest hope that the lessons in this book could help you prepare for your test successfully.

If you have any questions, please contact me at reza@effortlessmath.com and I will be glad to assist. Your feedback will help me to greatly improve the quality of my books in the future and make this book even better. Furthermore, I expect that I have made a few minor errors somewhere in this study guide. If you think this to be the case, please let me know so I can fix the issue as soon as possible.

If you enjoyed this book and found some benefit in reading this, I'd like to hear from you and hope that you could take a quick minute to post a review on the book's Amazon page. To leave your valuable feedback, please visit: amzn.to/2WnFQUo

Or scan this QR code.

I personally go over every single review, to make sure my books really are reaching out and helping students and test takers. Please help me help TSI Math test takers, by leaving a review!

I wish you all the best in your future success!

Reza Nazari

Math teacher and author

Made in United States
Orlando, FL
07 March 2024

44520871R00148